Rural Railways Series
Volume One

THE
HOLMFIRTH (SUMMER WINE) BRANCH LINE

Alan Earnshaw

NOSTALGIA
ROAD
PUBLICATIONS

CONTENTS

The **Rural Railway** Series ™

is produced under licence by

Nostalgia Road Publications Ltd.

Unit 6, Chancel Place

Shap Road Industrial Estate, Kendal LA9 6NZ

Tel. 01539 738832 - Fax: 01539 730075

designed and published by
Trans-Pennine Publishing Ltd.
PO Box 10, Appleby-in-Westmorland, Cumbria, CA16 6FA
Tel. 017683 51053 Fax. 017683 53558
e-mail: admin@transpenninepublishing.co.uk

and printed by
Kent Valley Colour Printers Ltd.
Kendal, Cumbria
01539 741344

© Trans-Pennine Publishing Ltd. 2005
Photographs: Author's collection or as credited

Front Cover: *Holmfirth in the mid-1950s; this specially commissioned watercolour by John Robinson is based on the title page picture. A strictly limited number of prints of this watercolour are available direct from the publishers.* **John Robinson**

Rear Cover Top: *This sepia tone picture is taken looking up towards the station, looking past the Victoria Hotel, which was once a popular hostelry for railwaymen and passengers alike, but has long since been demolished.* **Keith Longbottom**

Rear Cover Bottom: *Few pictures of Mytholmbridge Viaduct have emerged, except this colour image showing a three-coach train crossing the valley and heading towards the junction behind an LMS 2-6-4 tank.* **Keith Longbottom**

Title Page: *A typical working on the branch in 1955, sees one of Low Moor (Bradford) shed's 2-6-2Ts on a mid-day train. The usual three car Yorkshire branch set of coaches has been strengthened by the addition of an extra coach behind Ivatt 41250. Note the Piece Warehouse behind the locomotive.* **Real Photos**

This Page: *A view of Holmfirth Station from the turntable in the early 1930s, which clearly shows the ground frame lever and lamp hut.* **Francis Bray**

Above: *Still looking immaculate, Holmfirth sees the arrival of a Fowler 2-6-4T (42377) not long before the end of passenger services in 1959.* Peter Sunderland

INTRODUCTION

In this new Rural Railway series of books, we intend to present a view of some of those country railways promoted in the days of Queen Victoria, when railway mania was at its height. Many travelled into quite sparsely populated territory, others ventured through exceptionally difficult terrain. Both factors usually imparted to them their scenic natural beauty, but this was often coupled with the need for substantial feats of civil engineering.

Difficult to build and costly to operate, lines such as these were, a century or more later, to become victims to the infamous Dr. Beeching. In the guise of *The Re-Shaping Of British Railways* (a report published in 1963), thousands of miles of 'unprofitable' railways were swept away. Although a few lines remained, they in turn became just shadows of their former self, whilst a fortunate few were re-opened as preserved railways.

The problem with the Beeching report was the fact that it took no account of the fundamental truth that these little country lines provided much needed traffic for the system as a whole, and like a tree pruned of its branches, the remaining trunk would simply wither and slowly die. Yet in the hearts and minds of both enthusiasts and local people alike, these little rural railways live on. This series provides a timely reminder, lest we should forget.

To start the series, I would like to begin with the history of a small line in the former West Riding of Yorkshire, which at just over a mile in length had a history out of all proportion to its size; namely the Holmfirth Branch. The railway opened on 1st July 1850 and closed almost 115 years later on 3rd May 1965.

Above: *Although taken in British Railways days, this Aspinall 2-4-2T (50762) and the coaching stock behind it, is typical of the type of train that would run the Holmfirth to Huddersfield, Halifax or Bradford services. It is seen arriving from Holmfirth with a 'Yorkshire branch set'.* The late- Frank Alcock

The passenger services were officially withdrawn on Monday 2nd November 1959, though the last train had actually run on Saturday 31st October. I was still at primary school at Meltham Mills when that train ran, but I recall my father taking me on the Huddersfield Joint Omnibus Committee's number 35 bus route to witness the event, although I really did not understand what all the fuss was about. Yet I suspect the bribe of fish and chips from the 'chippy' in Hollowgate was sufficient enticement to brave the autumnal weather.

By the time the last goods train ran, in the Spring of 1965, I had moved on to Holmfirth High School and watched the railway's passing with more interest. Little did I appreciate then, that it was the victim of two pieces of Government-influenced policy. The first, and most important of these was the 1958 dictate that the railways had to achieve overall profitability within six years.

With the British Transport Commission owning 50% of the Huddersfield Joint Omnibus Committee it was easy to justify the passenger closure and hand the traffic to motor bus operation. Secondly, when stripped of its still profitable passenger trade, the branch had no chance of surviving the consequences of the Beeching Report issued in 1963. If many railways of the time were 'closed by stealth', Holmfirth was not one of them, its demise was an outright travesty, as it remained profitable down to the end.

Top Right: *Looking gaunt and austere, the immaculate station of 1959 has degenerated to a weed-strewn mess just three years later. The station buildings are still in use, but they now look as though nobody cares about them. The imposing Victorian buildings that formed the original station house and offices carry the typical brand marks of the industrial West Riding - soot blackened stonework.*

Bottom Right: *Things would get much worse before they got better. Yet, 30 years on from closure, this view from the Kingdom Hall on the former track-bed, shows just how nice the stonework would have looked when it was built in 1850.*

The derelict station and all the land was duly put up for sale by the British Railways Property Board, the asking price £2,875. Not only did this include all the station buildings, the goods warehouse and the stable block, but all the land as far back as Berry Banks.

If the then manager of the former Huddersfield Building Society's Holmfirth Branch should happen to be reading this book, I'd still like to know how he could refuse me a mortgage on the grounds that 'the site wasn't worth what the BRB were asking.' Thirty years on the majority of the old branch line has disappeared under new housing, and I will never forget the missed opportunity. At least the intervening years allowed me to study the line's history! So, in what has to be a pure piece of nostalgia, I hope you will enjoy my trip down memory lane.

Alan Earnshaw

Appleby-in-Westmorland,
April 2005

Politics And Plans

The story of the Holmfirth branch cannot be told in isolation, for it was just a small part of a much grander scheme to link the growing town of Huddersfield with Manchester, Sheffield and Leeds. Huddersfield and the surrounding districts had been settled since Neolithic times, but it was not until the 13th century that it began to develop as a textile manufacturing area.

With the coming of the industrial revolution, the area expanded to become the world's major centre for the manufacture of fine woollens and worsted cloth, and outlying communities like Holmfirth and New Mill were in the very centre of that development. As the industrial revolution progressed, they could ill-afford to be left behind and railways were therefore essential to progress.

Above: *Huddersfield is the focal point of the Holmfirth branch story and it eventually gained what is one of the finest railway buildings in Britain. This 1950s view shows the newly erected trolleybus shelters and the grime that obscured the fine facade for too many years.* Huddersfield Examiner

Shortly after the opening of the Stockton & Darlington Railway in 1825, proposals were made for a railway to link Huddersfield and Manchester, utilising the bed of the narrow canal passing through the Pennines at Standedge. Then, in 1834 there was again much talk of a railway being taken from Stalybridge to Huddersfield. The following year, 1835 saw a public meeting being held at the (old) George Hotel to discuss ways in which the town could be linked by rail to Leeds and Wakefield, but none of these early plans ever progressed!

As a consequence of public concern that the railway age was passing them by, a public meeting was called at the Court of Requests in Huddersfield on 17th January 1844. A deputation from the Manchester & Leeds Railway, headed by Captain Laws, attended to explain their views and proposals about a line that would follow the route of Sir John Ramsden's Canal into Huddersfield and terminate at Aspley. The meeting seemed to get off to a good start, as the M&L offered glowing praises about Huddersfield. Yet, their integrity was then challenged by a local businessman; he claimed "that the M&L could have instituted their line years before, but had never seen the necessity until the Sheffield & Manchester began talking about a line of their own." In reference to the proposed low-level terminus, another speaker shouted "they have clapped us in a hole and want to keep us there."

As a result of these fundamentally opposing views, little was achieved and the meeting ended without any real progress. Three months later the stalemate was still far from being resolved and as the letters, memorials and other petitions turned to frustration and criticism, the M&L retorted that "Huddersfield traffic was not worth stopping a train for." The town was in uproar, and with local feelings ruffled, the M&L scheme stood little chance when the plans were presented to Parliament later in the year. In turn a local company with the interests of Huddersfield at its heart was proposed, and as a result the Huddersfield Railway & Canal Company was founded. The local industrialists who were behind the scheme relied heavily on the expertise of the Sheffield, Ashton-under-Lyne & Manchester Railway (SA&MR), who it would join up with at Stalybridge.

Although it is outside the scope of this book, it must be said that neither the M&L (who later became the Lancashire & Yorkshire Railway) or the SA&MR (who eventually became Manchester, Sheffield & Lincolnshire Railway and finally the Great Central Railway) actually had any operational involvement with the Huddersfield to Manchester scheme, as the H&M formed an alliance with the Leeds, Dewsbury & Manchester Railway and in turn came to be operated by the London & North Western Railway.

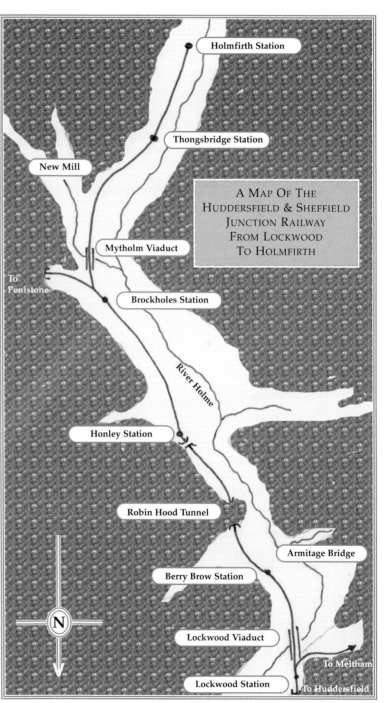

A MAP OF THE HUDDERSFIELD & SHEFFIELD JUNCTION RAILWAY FROM LOCKWOOD TO HOLMFIRTH

The concentrated effort on securing a Huddersfield to Manchester route left the Holme and Dearne valleys detached from the prospects of direct lines of communication and fearful of being left behind in this brave new era, local industrialists decided to promote a line for themselves. Despite the fact that the terrain south of Huddersfield did not readily lend itself to a railway, in 1843 a committee of 40 noted gentlemen had been selected to examine the feasibility of such a scheme. Early in 1844 they published their findings, showing that the railway might be achieved at a provisional cost of £30,000 per mile. The envisaged capital was to be £400,000, which they felt best to be subscribed in £50 shares. Encouraged by a favourable initial response from potential investors in Huddersfield, Sheffield, Leeds, Bradford and London, a prospectus was issued on 23rd September 1844.

Unfortunately, from a historian's point of view this document is most ambiguous, promoting a theory rather than specifying a route. Perhaps this is due to the fact that at that time a choice of routes was available. The first passed across the River Colne to Lockwood and then followed the Holme Valley on to Honley and then went up to New Mill, where it would cut through the high ridge at Thurstonland before progressing on to Shepley. The other route also reached Shepley, but did so via easier terrain, following a line from Huddersfield through Dalton and the Kirkburton Valley. Because there is no firm set of plans on which to base our projection of the proposed routes, we have to surmise which way it would have gone. The most likely common meeting point of these two proposals would have been somewhere close to what later became Clayton West Junction. From thereon, the route of both proposals would have followed common ground all the way to SA&MR's new line over Woodhead with which they would make a junction at Penistone.

Unable to decide between the merits each route would offer, the committee approached the SA&MR for their advice on this point. William Brook, a Meltham cotton-spinner, was asked to represent the committee at a meeting with the railway in Sheffield. The process must have been a lengthy one, for it was not until 28th October 1845 that Brook reported back to the committee, advising them that "the H&SJR should favour the Holme Valley as it would pass through the most inhabited parts of the district." Yet, despite the extra revenue this offered, the New Mill option would also be the most costly to create.

In fact, there would be exceptionally heavy engineering work, including at least six viaducts and five long tunnels. Such was Victorian optimism however, that this did not deter the provisional committee who resolved that the scheme "should proceed by a route, which on examination, should appear the best, most direct and accommodate the greatest number of population." Evidently, finance was not a major consideration! The next stage was the surveying, but Joseph Locke and Alfred Stanistreet Jee were already preparing plans and sections using measurements that had been prepared for earlier proposals.

The plans were taken to a meeting of the provisional committee on 11th November 1845, and discussed over a cold collation costing 4s 3d (21p) per head. The outline plans were well received; the chairman stating "not only do they serve the greater needs of the communities spread hither through the Holme Valley, but much cheer should be expressed that the overall cost would be reduced." This cost reduction however, was achieved at not taking the line through New Mill, for it was now intended to curve into the Thurstonland Ridge just after Brockholes. By way of compensation, a new branch line would now be built to Holmfirth with an intermediate station at Thongsbridge, which was "nobbut a mile from the New Mills." In addition to ignoring 'the New Mills', the communities at Kirkburton, Skelmanthorpe and Clayton West were also to be excluded. Though a tentative suggestion was made "for branch lines to these places at a later date", the H&SJR's failure to serve the interests of these communities very nearly led to encroachments by other railway companies in later years, most seriously the LNWR and the Midland.

Though these communities felt aggrieved at their exclusion from the projected route, the published proposals attracted only two objections. One of these was quickly withdrawn, but the other came from an elderly lady who claimed £6,000 compensation for the loss of part of her garden that would be needed for the construction of the railway. The land was valued at just £300, but the rest was claimed as being compensation for the inconvenience. The company offered £2,000, but this was rejected. Though the matter was amicably settled later, no record of the precise sum was ever disclosed. However, from a study of the documentation in the House of Lords Record Office, it can be determined that she was one of the three individuals, who each received sums in excess of £2,000 for 'inconvenience'; nobody was paid a sum of £6,000.

The matter must have been dealt with speedily, because the same records show that Parliament were advised that the Bill was unopposed and "all matters pertaining to land and liberty have been satisfied", when it went before the House for its third reading on 28th May 1845.

Royal Assent was granted by Queen Victoria on 30th June the same year. Interestingly, during the passage through Parliament, the Secretary of the Board of Trade specifically commended Jee on the neatness of his plans and their accuracy. A set of those plans in the author's possession confirm that this praise was not misplaced. Furthermore, not only was the scheme very well received in Parliament, but it also went down well in the financial institutions of London.

Top Right: *Working the branch often fell to locomotives from Bradford's Low Moor shed, which by tradition is attributed to Thomas Normington. In the 1850s he reputedly suggested that the trains from Bradford or Halifax to Huddersfield be extended to Penistone or Holmfirth, thus doing away with the necessity of relying on MS&LR engines. After the Grouping, some Holmfirth branch trains were operated by the ex-LNWR shed at Hillhouse, and on 10th September 1950, a 2-6-2T (41267) gets ready for a freight working to the branch.*

Bottom Right: *The branch was mostly worked by 2-4-2T, 2-6-2 and 2-6-4 tank engines, or 0-6-0 tender engines, but smaller locomotives would also be used. Having just returned from the Holmfirth branch, ex-L&YR Barton-Wright 0-6-0T (11447) shunts the Fitzwilliam Street Goods Yard in Huddersfield in 1949.*
The late Frank Alcock

Some 520 local investors had already pledged £37,000, but it will be recalled that the total requirement was £400,000 so this did not even represent 10% of what was required. But the City had no difficulty with the floatation, nor did finance houses in Manchester and Newcastle. Further monies were raised in Barnsley, Bradford, Halifax, Leeds and Sheffield. Inside a month 106 subscribers had put up a further £106,000, and more had taken out options on further stock. Meanwhile, work on the eastern section of the SA&MR was then nearing completion, and the line opened between Sheffield and Dunford Bridge without any formality on 14th July.

In so doing' it created the link from Sheffield, which would provide the means for construction of the H&SJR. Indeed, even though the SA&MR was still working on Woodhead Tunnel, it would appear that much of the SA&MR's equipment was disposed of to the H&SJR Board. Some 236 navvies previously engaged between Dunford and Sheffield, were also to find employment on the line between Huddersfield and Penistone or the Holmfirth branch line. It must be appreciated that the Huddersfield & Sheffield Junction Railway Company, was only ever intended as a promotional organisation, and it never had any pretensions towards actually operating the line itself. This is clearly demonstrated in Section 35 of the Act, which allowed for the line to be leased to the M&L, SA&MR, Midland or even Manchester & Birmingham, or a combination of any two of these companies.

It may seem odd that the latter two companies are mentioned, but it has to be remembered that the SA&MR had not sufficiently recovered from its financial difficulties incurred during the Woodhead construction, and there was a proposal that the company should be absorbed jointly by the M&B and the Midland. Ultimately this could have meant that the H&SJR could have passed into railways that would have later become the Great Central, London & North Western or Midland, instead of the Lancashire & Yorkshire Railway as it eventually transpired.

By the provisions of Section 35, the SA&MR saw the opportunity to reach Huddersfield and Holmfirth. They also felt that by offering technical support to both the H&SJR and the H&M, that the commercial interests in the area would become receptive to their overtures. Their offer of technical support to the H&M was readily accepted, so Locke and Jee were instructed to prepare plans and sections for the route to Manchester.

The first formal meeting of the H&SJR Board was held in Huddersfield's Guildhall on 31st July 1845, when all present were told that the new line would be open inside 30 months. In addition to an exceptionally optimistic opening date, there appears to have been a great deal of underestimating of the actual construction costs.

Yet perhaps all were swept along with the euphoria of the day. The line, as finally estimated would cost £531,258 and the authorised capital was £532,000. The differential between the two sums seems awfully small, and one of the new Directors, Joseph Armitage, a cotton-spinning mill owner, shocked his board when he made a similar comment in 1846 - no doubt compounding the horror when he said a further £60,000 might be needed.

Another person who the SA&MR asked to help the H&M was my great-great-great-grandfather, Thomas Nicholson, who had been the contractor on the Dunford Bridge end of the new Woodhead Tunnel. Gaining invaluable experience in dealing with the terrain, the SA&MR recommended that if the H&M were to cut through the Pennines at Standedge, it was recognised that he was by far the best man for the job.

According to Thomas Nicholson's diary much of the survey work had already been done in connection with the earlier SA&MR proposals. Nicholson got the job at Standedge and the SA&MR connived to get A. S. Jee's younger brother, Morland Jee, appointed as the H&M's resident engineer for the 3-mile long tunnel. Furthermore, it is also obvious that much of the land for both the H&M and H&SJR schemes had already been purchased.

Although both projects were to proceed simultaneously, the Manchester line was seen as being paramount, and on 31st July the H&SJR board decided that the construction of the H&M between Heaton Lodge and Huddersfield was more important and they acquiesced to a request from the H&M board for "the release of the services of A. S. Jee." This is not surprising when the respective members of the two company Boards are compared, as there were a great many common denominators.

They even had the same Chairmen and Vice-Chairmen, the first of these was the industrialist Joseph Armitage, who was appointed as the H&SJR Chairman and many subsequent 'short' board meetings would be held at his home Milnsbridge House at Thornton Lodge in the future. His vice-Chairman was C. H. Jones who, in 1868, would become the first Mayor of Huddersfield.

On the H&M Board, Armitage's and Jones' roles were reversed. It was very much a "brotherly atmosphere" wrote Nicholson, in his diary in June 1845 "Armitage and Jones, Jones and Armitage, I never knew to whom I should doff my hat first. More was accomplished by a nod and a wink, and nary a handshake between them.........they knew what was wanted, and happen nobody else did, but they would never let on. Poor Mister Jee was oft led a merry dance, for it was certain that the communications with Manchester was what they wanted most."

Above: *Photographs from the early years of the line's operation are simply not available, so those displayed on the pages that follow take the reader on a brief pictorial journey from Huddersfield to Brockholes. This view shows that, although Huddersfield station looked imposing from St. George's Square, what lay behind was less impressive. In this view, taken before 1916, an L&YR 2-4-2T (661) simmers in the west end island bay as its driver reads the newspaper. This tank engine was the one lost in a fall from the Penistone Viaduct when it collapsed in 1916. Bamforth*

Nicholson records this in his diary, stating (of Leeds and Sheffield) "they could wait till kingdom cometh for all they (Armitage and Jones) were to seem concerned at, at times."

Perhaps the request that the H&SJR release their engineers was a mere formality, for the records show that he was appointed on 29th July anyway, a full two days before the H&SJR meeting. As it was, Jee was not totally at the beck and call of the H&M, and his role was more of a consultant working in an advisory capacity. In reality, most of the site work fell on the shoulders of his younger brother, who was in fact appointed as the Resident Engineer at a salary of £800pa.

Nicholson records the events, writing "Morland is a good fellow, but has his fancies which I do not always hold with - he has angered Mr. Brook no end of times by his fastidiousness and petulance, but that man can deal with cotton spinners, and can shout over the top of any machine so he will get his way with Jee in time."

Despite the efforts being placed on the Leeds – Huddersfield – Manchester route, the H&SJR scheme had by no means been allowed to languish, and the Right Hon. Lord Wharncliffe, Lord President of Her Majesty's Privy Council, cut the first sod at the southern end of Wellhouse Cutting near Penistone on 29th August 1845. The Earl's connections with the SA&MR were very strong and, in addition to his shareholdings in that enterprise, he had cut the first sod at Woodhead in 1838. Seven years later his health was in a poor state, but "he regaled himself and accepted the invitation heartily."

It should perhaps be mentioned that Wharncliffe was to die a few months later, on 19th December - three days before the official opening of the whole Woodhead route. Nicholson recalls his passing "t'was a sad day however, for amidst all the triumphal arches and backslapping, many wore black ribbons on their coat sleeves. His Lordship had always shown great favour to the conditions of the men, and many a navvy was in tears at his passing."

Within a few days of Wharncliffe's death most of the men were gone, even though much work was yet to start on the Penistone to Huddersfield railway. Nicholson wrote, "In need of wages they went on the trod to other works, many in Wales or Cumberland, and but few remained whence the [Woodhead] line was fully opened. Of those who remained, bricklayers, pullers and platemen etc.; there were, at the opening ceremony, a great many who drank to his Lordship's memory rather than to the railway."

The H&SJR ceremony in August had in fact, been one of Wharncliffe's last public duties but he took the lead in the speech-making wishing "prosperity to the undertaking." Speaking of the celebrations, the *Penistone Almanac* records "The carriages that were used [by the SA&MR] to convey the guests to Penistone were hardly dignified, as they were somewhat similar to an uncovered cattle truck."

A procession was led by a local band, and afterwards a 'sumptuous tea' was provided in Penistone Church School-room. Presided over by Joseph Armitage, the celebrations went on until 7pm - a fact recorded by the various caterers' bills. For example the bill for lunch at the Rose & Crown Inn, Penistone, was as follows:

	£	s	d
80 Gents lunches @ 5/-	20	0	0
44 bottles of champagne @ 10/-	22	0	0
41 bottles of port @ 5/6d	11	5	6
39 bottles of sherry @ 5/6d	10	14	6
3 bottles of soda water @ 6d	1	6	0
13 bottles of soda water @ 6d	6	6	0
6 quarts of ale & porter @ 6d	19	9	0
Meat, &c for Mr. Miller's Men	7	0	0
Broken Glasses		4	0
Doorkeeper		3	0
Total	72	17	9

Cheque to settle £70.

With the celebrations out of the way, Mr. Miller (the contractor) began working from three principal construction sites, Penistone, Gunthwaite and Springwood Junction (see picture opposite). The resident engineer had an office at what became the Springwood sidings, but it is later believed that he moved locations and built some sort of office wherever the greater work was being carried out; as for example the cottages erected alongside Woodhead Road at the south end of Lockwood Viaduct.

Right: *This picture at Springwood Junction on Saturday 8th August 1959 will be quite familiar to anyone who ever travelled along the H&SJR, or any of its three branch lines. Here a Fowler 2-6-4 tank engine heads on to what had once been the starting point of the isolated section of the L&YR system. The engine 42384 is based at Hillhouse, and the first two carriages are typical branch stock, but the third one is an LMS corridor third-brake. The siding in the foreground served the coal drops at Springwood. The late Reverend Eric Treacy*

Left: *Here we see an Ivatt 2-6-2T working tender-first to Holmfirth as it approaches Yews Hill (Lockwood) Tunnel having just crossed Paddock Viaduct. This was one mile from the point where the H&SJR (L&YR) diverged from the H&M (LNWR) line at Springwood, which was originally envisaged as an underground junction. The practice of tank locomotives working bunker-out, smokebox-back was common on all the branches of the H&SJR in LMS and BR days; although Holmfirth was an exception when the turntable was in operation.* Kenneth Field

As work progressed on both the H&SJR and the H&M, the SA&MR continued with its attempt to acquire the lease for both these lines when they were finally completed. However, all was not running smoothly, and on 27th September a serious Boardroom row developed between the SA&MR-sponsored members and the Huddersfield interests. The M&L, keen to exploit the growing rift, stepped in and began courting both sides realising it had probably missed out on a 'good thing' when it turned it's back on Huddersfield in 1843-4.

There was obviously a good deal of politicking going on. For example, following a meeting at Milnsbridge House (date not recorded - but probably shortly after the full opening of the Woodhead line) it became apparent that the SA&MR's ultimate goal was a route from Manchester and Sheffield to Leeds and not Huddersfield as had originally been promulgated.

Now, despite their close proximity, there has always been something of a rivalry between Huddersfield and Leeds (a trait still noted today in terms of football support), and there was never very much love lost between the two. Therefore, the secret intentions of the SA&MR Board rubbed against the grain of this ill-feeling. Many years later vice-Chairman Jones is reported to have said, "the SA&MR saw us [the H&SJR] as a means to an end, but their end was not Huddersfield, but Leeds."

This feeling was obviously manifest in a number of ways, and there was a great deal of suspicion about the SA&MR's motivation. With this in mind, after a seven-hour-long meeting held on 28th February 1846, the H&M shareholders rejected an SA&MR take-over proposal by a small majority. The resolution of the board being that "the H&M would maintain, for the time being, its independence from the SA&MR, M&L and the LNWR" who were all expressing an interest in the town.

However, so slender was the majority against the SA&MR take-over of the H&M, that the Sheffield-company renewed their efforts to reach Huddersfield through the H&SJR. To an extent this remained the easier alternative, because they already had five directors provisionally elected on to the H&SJR's Board.

Had the SA&MR left it at that, then the colour of Huddersfield's railway map may well have been completely different to what it eventually became. But, with complete over-confidence, the SA&MR began to contrive secret alliances with other railways over traffic sharing. About this time plans for a Halifax, Huddersfield & Bradford Union Railway were being promoted, with the support of the West Riding Union Railway, which in turn was somewhat ironically supported by the M&L. It was with the HH&BUR that the SA&MR made its first alliance, but there could be no doubt that the deals were being done with the M&L and others.

This act, when discovered, again enraged local interests who began to question, if this was the case "whether they had need for the SA&MR at all?" Indeed, it can be demonstrated that the SA&MR's under-hand tactics had back-fired on them, because many influential people in Huddersfield now felt that "the HH&BUR's proposals were of greater benefit to them." Accordingly, the H&SJR began an open association with the HH&BUR.

This led to a serious deterioration in the relationship between the H&SJR board and the SA&MR, particularly after the Directors' meeting on 27th September 1845 when the M&L had stepped in to the fray by offering 10,640 £50 M&L shares for H&SJR stock. Meanwhile, in 1847 the M&L changed its name to the Lancashire & Yorkshire Railway as a reflection of the much greater area it then covered. In the same year the SA&MR became the Manchester, Sheffield & Lincolnshire Railway and the Manchester & Birmingham, Leeds, Dewsbury & Manchester and H&M railways joined the newly formed London & North Western (LNWR).

Having lost its influence in the Huddersfield area, the MS&LR became difficult about offering the L&YR connections at Penistone. This was essential as the end of the H&SJR line terminated at a junction with the MS&LR that was some distance east of the town's station, and L&YR trains needed to reverse 'wrong line' to reach the platforms. Clearly the matter needed to be resolved as a matter of urgency, if the H&SJR was not going to become a railway to nowhere.

Top Left: *Although it may sound ridiculous to say so today, once upon a time Lockwood was a fashionable resort spa, and the trains carried visitors from all over the north. From the Down (Penistone-bound) platform, a carriage drive led to Swan Lane, such was the volume of carriages that came to meet the trains. If you find this hard to believe, the cobbled sets of the carriage road can still be seen. The 'swan-neck' water column seen on the right of the picture, originally came from Blackpool. The water tank at the far end of the Up platform was fed by a system of cast-iron pipes carrying spring-water from the Butternab area along the Meltham Branch.* B. C. Lane Collection

Bottom Left: *A view of John Hawkshaw's mighty Lockwood Viaduct, viewed from Beaumont Park.*

The MS&LR were only placated when the L&YR entered into an interim agreement allowing them to work trains over the entire length of the H&SJR and the Holmfirth branch. In January 1848 a more formal agreement allowed the MS&LR to work a Holmfirth to Penistone passenger service (once it opened), and have the opportunity to work goods services into Huddersfield.

In return the L&YR were granted running powers to Sheffield for both passenger and goods trains, but even so this still meant that the whole of the H&SJR section had no physical connection with any other part of the L&YR system and its early operation was consequently fraught with problems.

At the Huddersfield end, these were resolved when the L&YR gained running powers over the LNWR line between Heaton Lodge and Huddersfield Joint Station. This allowed them contact with the rest of the L&YR system, and their main line to Leeds or Manchester.

The MS&LR's running powers to Holmfirth and the traffic sharing were far less satisfactory, and (as recorded later) many complaints appeared about it in both the Huddersfield and Sheffield newspapers.

I believe that MS&LR locomotives did work the branch at first, but this was probably only a temporary state of affairs caused by a distinct shortage of locomotives on the L&YR system at that time. Detailed searches of the railway minute books give no clues, nor do they confirm the existence of a reputed south-facing spur at the junction, which allowed Holmfirth branch trains direct access to Penistone.

Folklore also suggests that an engine shed existed at Holmfirth in the early years. But despite extensive research into the subject, I cannot confirm this. It is more likely that an engine was stabled there overnight, or perhaps the contractors may have had a temporary shed for their engine during the building of the line - but again there is no official record of this.

Top Right: *A view of Berry Brow in L&YR days with a Barton-Wright 0-6-0 tender engine calling with a pick-up goods train from Lockwood to Holmfirth.* Barry C. Lane collection

Bottom Right: *An excellent study of a typical scene on the H&SJR line in BR days. The location, on the north side of Honley Tunnel is less common, and 42409 is in a section of the route that was exceptionally difficult to build. The exposed shale on the left of the engine will reveal why the builders wanted to abandon their original plans for this section, and replace the cutting with a tunnel instead.* Peter Sunderland

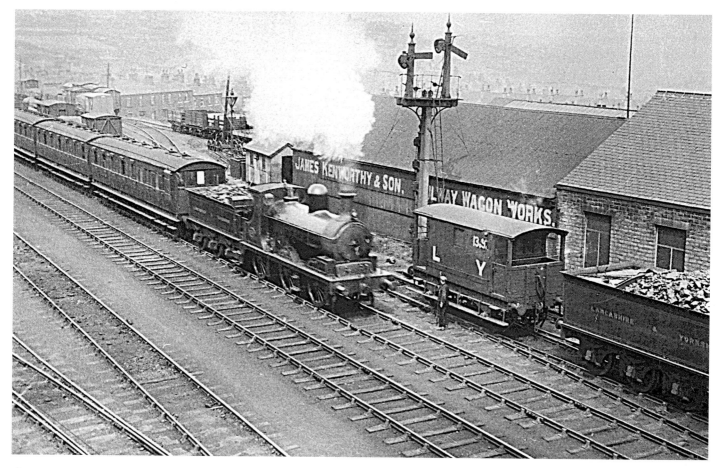

INAUGURAL SERVICES

Following the opening of the eastern section of the Woodhead route in 1845, a horse-drawn bus service was introduced jointly by the L&YR and the MS&LR to connect the railway at Penistone with Huddersfield and Holmfirth.

However, when the H&M (LNWR) opened in the summer of 1847, the L&YR withdrew from this arrangement and offered a railway service to Normanton where connections could be gained to the Leeds - Sheffield trains. The MS&LR then altered its horse-bus service to a journey that connected Dunford Bridge Station with Holmfirth and Huddersfield, and thus offered a quicker connection to Manchester than anything previously available.

Above: *Once again, we have no photographs of the line that date from the Victorian era, so this section utilises the earliest pictures that have thus far come to light. Here a Barton Wright 0-6-0 tender locomotive passes Kenworthy's Wagon Works at Lockwood, whilst en-route to Holmfirth.* Jack Adamson

This bus left the Boot & Shoe Inn on Huddersfield's New Street at 6.30am and 1.15pm, taking an hour to reach Holmfirth. The buses arrived at Dunford Bridge at 8.30am and 3.15pm respectively, where connections were advertised to Manchester, Sheffield, Nottingham and Grimsby. The horse-bus returned to Huddersfield 20 minutes after its arrival times in Dunford Bridge, though in April 1850 one journey was curtailed near Honley when the coach suffered a broken axle.

This accident demonstrated that the over-worked bus was just about ready for retirement, and until the H&SJR opened in July a replacement service was operated on behalf of the MS&LR by James Siddell-Lockwood of Meltham. This was my great-great-grandfather (and the son-in-law of Thomas Nicholson), and the award of the contract to him undoubtedly smacks of nepotism - or was this just Victorian enterprise?

By May the H&SJR was complete, except for what is described as signalling installation. What type of signalling this would have been remains unclear, as it was very early for the type of signals we would recognise today. However, as Thomas Swinburn (who the L&YR appointed as their engineer) was an undoubted genius in the art of signalling and point design, so perhaps his work on the H&SJR led to a safety system that was much more sophisticated than has otherwise been appreciated?

Top Right: *Early in the LMS-era, another Aspinall 2-4-2T comes off the Holmfirth branch at Brockholes Junction with a rake of L&YR 'Yorkshire Branch' stock. This locomotive (10797) was based at Goole (23C) for most of its working life.* Jack Adamson

Bottom Right: *A wonderful view taken of the 'in-filled' bay platform under the canopy between the 1890 booking office and the Piece Warehouse in the 1930s. The view shows an elderly gent (perhaps an ancestor of the stoic Clegg from* Last of the Summer Wine) *as he waits with his terrier on a long bench suitably lettered LMS Holmfirth! Note the many adverts on the wall behind.*
Percy Shaw, courtesy Francis Bray

Though the Holmfirth branch was promoted as an integral part of the H&SJR, there are strong grounds to believe that it was intended that the line from Huddersfield to Holmfirth would open long before the rest of the system. Such a view is specifically reinforced by the fact that as early as 1848 the L&YR were advising local textile mills of the services which would be provided in "the very near future." The fact that the L&YR did not commence Holmfirth traffic ahead of the opening of the whole route is only attributable to the delays in completing Paddock Viaduct, the first major structure on the H&SJR.

If these delays had not occurred with the crossing of the Colne Valley, it would have been an eminently logical move to get traffic running from Holmfirth to Huddersfield at an early stage, thus allowing the railway to begin earning much-needed revenue. Indeed, we know that most of the line was completed well before the end of 1849, and with the exception of the viaduct, only a "few minor works were required to permit the inauguration of a Holmfirth - Lockwood service."

The completeness of the works is noted by a report in a local paper in February 1850, which stated that the only aspect of the line to complete were the "finishing touches" of the station house, and it is possible that these delays were due to the harsh winter weather that had been experienced at the end of 1849. Another form of evidence is highlighted by a case that came before Holmfirth Magistrates' Court early in April 1850 when Joseph Graves and George Ingham appeared before the bench on a charge of trespassing on the railway.

In evidence the two defendants stated that they were keen ramblers and had been in the habit of walking along the railway every Sunday for some time and they did not know that what they were doing was in breach of the law. They also added that though the works were completed there had been no trace of workmen for several months [probably since the previous summer]. In reply, Mr. Ashton for the contractors, Miller & Co., stated that with the railway being complete and now almost ready for trains to be run upon it, the railway were desirous of stopping trespassers who were using the railway as a short cut to Thongsbridge and Honley.

The magistrate looked at the case sympathetically and the two were let off with a friendly caution, though it was forcibly pointed out to them that they could have faced a £10 fine.

It was then planned that the line would open on 24th June 1850, with a celebration to be held at the house of Mr. Dyson at 7pm. When this failed to happen it was said that the branch would open with the main line on 1st July 1850, and the first public passenger train would leave from Holmfirth at 11.25am. The opening ceremony was well attended, despite the fact that it was an atrociously wet day. The first train ran from Huddersfield, behind an MS&LR locomotive hauling an excursion to Rowsley.

The price of the tickets 13s (65P) first class and 6s 6d (32.5p) included a horse-drawn coach ride to the Duke of Devonshire's stately home and admission to Chatsworth House and its grounds. It was a rare treat for people from a textile town to visit a stately home of such grandeur, and there is little wonder that the train was so well patronised. It is often widely quoted that this train originated at Holmfirth; in fact it did nothing of the sort because there actually were two 'first trains'. And, though it forms no part of the Holmfirth story, it is well worth recounting.

Unfortunately the train provided from Huddersfield was insufficient for all those who had presented themselves at the station, and it was known that many more would be waiting at the intermediate stations on the line, including a large number who were due to get off the first Holmfirth train at Brockholes. Accordingly Mr. Hall, the L&YR's Traffic Manager found a number of extra coaches, possibly having them taken off another train at Mirfield. In the midst of a downpour (and to the accompaniment of a band) the MS&LR locomotive pulled away from Huddersfield somewhat behind schedule and entered the tunnel. After "an atrocious spinning of the wheels" it emerged at Springwood, from where it progressed southwards over Paddock Viaduct.

More people boarded at Lockwood, Berry Brow and Honley, but there was insufficient room for all those waiting at Brockholes. The MS&LR engine was, by then seriously overburdened and it made a difficult start from Brockholes, slipping badly before it managed to gain adhesion. Just ahead lay Stocks Moor (Thurstonland) Tunnel, which was always a notoriously wet subterranean passage. As a consequence of this and the train's heavy load, it came to a halt midway through the tunnel and was unable to restart. The steam from the engine blasted against the roof and, as this condensed in to dirty sooty water, it only added to the misery of passengers who were in the open carriages.

The only option was to divide the train in half, so the front portion was taken on to the level section of track at Stocksmoor Station with the intention that the engine would then return for the second half. One can only imagine the discomfort of those left behind in the tunnel for 25 minutes, but few would have realised that they had been left in a position that was far more dangerous than was immediately evident.

At the same time as the Rowsley excursion left Huddersfield at 11.25am, the first Holmfirth branch train was scheduled to leave its terminus destined first for Huddersfield. From early in the morning church bells throughout the Holme Valley tolled to signal the importance of the day. A well-known local Master of Ceremonies, Mr. James Bates of Winnay Bank, conducted the proceedings and the Holmfirth Band played a series of melodies on the station platform.

Top Right: *Although the two views on this page are of inferior quality, and taken from Bamforth & Co postcards, they do show two interesting early-20th century views. The upper shot looks across the valley to the station goods yard and coal drops (note a complete absence of trees on the embankment). A Barton-Wright 0-6-0 tender engine can just be made out, as can private owner coal wagons belonging to Sir John Kaye (Emley Moor Colliery), Holmfirth Gas Light Co., Holmfirth Co-op and Ben Hardy (Holmfirth). Note the original layout of the coal cells.*

Bottom Right: *A Barton-Wright 0-6-0 tank engine runs around its train on the terminal platform as a full complement of station staff look on.* both Bamforth

Despite the shortness of this journey a locomotive and 14 carriages left the branch, with the band now placed in two open carriages at the front. They played all the way to Huddersfield ignoring the torrential rain and only pausing when the train ran through the various tunnels encountered en-route. On arrival at Huddersfield a military band, which had given the civic send-off to the 11.25am departure, was waiting to welcome the Holmfirth train. This train then formed a 12-noon departure for Penistone, where once again its arrival was met by yet another band. The day was declared a local holiday in the Holme Valley and passengers were allowed unlimited travel over the whole of the H&SJR line and the Holmfirth branch for a single fare. Trains ran at regular intervals throughout the day, and it was well after dusk when the last passengers alighted, as many of them had attended a celebration held by the contractors Miller, Blackie & Shortridge at the Rose & Crown Inn Penistone.

The majority of the passengers however, returned to Holmfirth on the 3.32pm from Penistone in order to get back for the celebratory tea that had been planned in connection with the opening ceremony. During the first week a total of 1,869 tickets were sold at Holmfirth Station, with 674 at the intermediate station of Thongsbridge. However just twelve days after the line opened it was marred by tragedy, when a newly-married man named Vautry hung himself from Mytholmbridge Viaduct whilst in a state of intoxication.

Below: *This picture of Aspinall 2-4-2T (10873) from Mirfield shed, is fascinating because it shows that the platform canopy had already been removed in front of the Piece Warehouse before it was taken in October 1947. As the warehouse was last used in 1953, the picture proves that the two were not demolished together in the early 1950s as has long been quoted in previous material written about the branch. Francis Bray*

BROCKHOLES AND THE JUNCTION

At just 1 mile 65 chains long it may be wondered if there was a need for the line at all. Yet its construction can be best viewed by keeping in mind the thought that this was intended to be the first stage of a much longer route to the west. In 1847, prior to the opening, an Act of Parliament was obtained to extend the line through to Holmbridge at a cost of £56,000.

Though these powers were allowed to lapse in 1852, it was just one of a series of proposals to extend the line beyond Holmfirth. These were repeated in 1873, but with no progress obvious two years later, the Chief Constable headed a deputation to Manchester with the intention of persuading the L&YR General Manager. A promise that the matter would be "looked into" produced nothing, though the proposals were raised repeatedly, especially in the years 1879, 1881 and 1890 in line with local expectations.

Above: *This view shows Brockholes Junction station some time after the numerous station improvements that were influenced by repeated Board of Trade criticism of the train working here. To be fair, these improvements also came about from a desire to specifically improve the branch services too, and were also carried out at Thongsbridge and Holmfirth in this period. Note the signalbox just beyond the end of the right-hand platform; it was a 25-lever L&YR 'box, but was up-rated to a 30-lever frame in LMS days.* Bamforth

That the L&YR had intended to extend the line cannot be doubted, for the branch was laid as double track throughout. When this is compared with Clayton West's single track (aimed at an extension to Barnsley), it shows just how positive the extension proposals were. Various schemes envisaged the line extending up the Holme Valley before tunnelling below Holme Moss, then connecting with MS&LR's mainline around Crowden in the Etherow Valley.

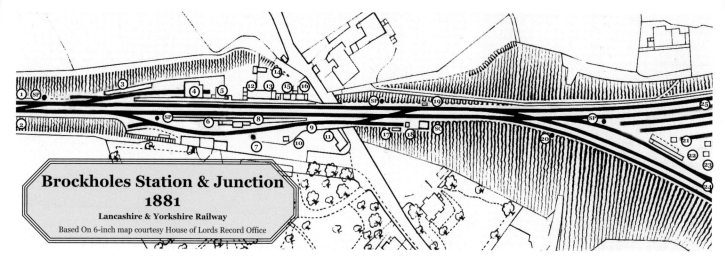

Brockholes Station & Junction
1881
Lancashire & Yorkshire Railway
Based On 6-inch map courtesy House of Lords Record Office

MAP OF 1881		MAP OF 1921	
	12 Stationmaster's House.		12 Stationmaster's House
	13 Booking Office &		13 Booking Office &
SC Signal Cabin	13a Waiting/Lamp Rooms	SC Signal Cabin	13a Waiting Room
SP Signal Post	14 Weigh House	SP Signal Post	14 Weigh House
1 To Huddersfield	15 Water tank	1 To Huddersfield	15 Water tank
2 Original cross-over	16 District PW Office	2 New cross-over	16 Engineer's Offices
3 Loading stage	17 SC Coal Stage	3 Old loading stage	17 SC Coal Stage
4 Goods Warehouse	18 S&T Store	4 Armitage & Co store.	18 S&T Store/Closet
5 Brockholes Co-op shed	19 S&T Office	5 Footbridge	19 S&T Department
6 Up shelter	20 Permanent Way Hut	6 Up waiting room	20 Permanent Way Hut
7 Yard Crane (hand)	21 C&W Inspector	7 Yard Crane (hand)	21 C&W Hut
8 Porter's room	22 PW Loading Ramp	8 Porters/lamp room	22 Old Loading Ramp
9 Coal drops	23 Loop line	9 Coal drops	23 Crippled wagon road
10 Merchant's office	24 To Holmfirth	10 Merchant's offices	24 To Holmfirth
11 Cartage Dept./Stables	25 To Penistone	11 Cartage Dept./Stables	25 To Penistone

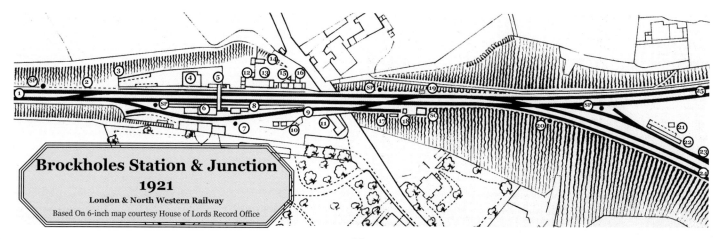

Brockholes Station & Junction
1921
London & North Western Railway
Based On 6-inch map courtesy House of Lords Record Office

Top Right: *A visit to Brockholes station today will not show how important this junction once was! However, I trust that these maps and pictures will give an impression of its former glory. The station was originally called Holmfirth Junction, and later it became Brock Holes Junction and finally just Brockholes. This view, looking towards Huddersfield dates from the mid-1920s, and is dated by the locomotive chimney pot and the LMS notice boards. The former wooden goods warehouse is seen still standing behind and to the right of the footbridge. Note the large compliment of station staff.* Francis Bray

Bottom Right: *This view of Brockholes station looking south, clearly shows the junction . A water column, water tank and junction signal are seen on the right, the signal box is on the left. In the distance the junction sidings are full of wagons. In the 1850s it is believed that this was once a triangular junction, and aerial photography by the Royal Air Force in 1948 reveals that at some stage there had been a curve leading from the branch on to the Penistone-bound line, although it had a very sharp radius. One letter in the Sheffield press implies that such a curve was used by trains running from Sheffield to Holmfirth. No further evidence has been presented to either substantiate or refute this claim, but if true, it would explain why connections were missed at the junction station. The junction was later reduced to just a south-facing arm and Brockholes became the meeting point for the L&YR's Huddersfield-Holmfirth trains and MS&LR's Penistone-Holmfirth service. Even so it was fraught with problems, but the 'joint arrangement' was scrapped, probably within a few years.* Bamforth, courtesy B. C. Lane Collection

Top Left: *Brockholes Junction as a Stanier 2-6-4T (42622) heads down the branch in June 1958. This Saturday-only train has an eclectic mixture of corridor and compartment stock. In the V of the junction, the course of one of the former Engineer's Sidings can be traced by the remaining set of buffer stops.* Peter Sunderland

Bottom Left: *Pulled up outside the Brockholes Junction Cabin, 90325 is a Riddles Austerity (an ex-WD 8F 2-8-0) based at Huddersfield Hillhouse Shed (55G).* Harold Armitage

As the station's traffic became mainly passenger-related, the goods facilities on the 'Penistone' side were not fully utilised, so when 'junction' improvements were introduced in the early-1880s, freight trains were limited to a loop off the Huddersfield-bound line on which three coal cells were located. In 1884 the station was enlarged with the main platforms being lengthened at the expense of the warehouse and bay platform, which became part of the stationmaster's garden. Other improvements included a footbridge, installed so that passengers could cross the busy line without having to use the barrow crossing.

From Brockholes the Holmfirth line headed almost due south in a gentle curve, running to one side of land that housed the Civil Engineer's and Carriage & Wagon Dept.'s sidings. Three sidings ran parallel with the line from Penistone, and one of these was used to house the District Engineer's train and inspection carriage, which was usually pulled on its travels by the Brockholes Junction 'pilot engine'. Three more sidings ran off from the south end of the Holmfirth loop, the capacity of which was extended in 1916 to hold 331 wagons. This huge area was situated on a substantial embankment, but the western side of this was the most substantial. The bulk of the material that made up the 'infill' having been taken from the excavations for Thurstonland Tunnel, the western portal for which was just a few hundred yards east of the junction area.

At the southern end, the loop rejoined the Holmfirth-bound line around the point where it crossed Oaks Lane by an over-bridge. After the junction and sidings had been left behind, the line traversed a cutting spanned first by an occupation bridge and then by the bridge carrying the road to Thurstonland. Emerging from the cutting it crossed the New Mill road and then ran on to a small embankment leading to the 13-arch Mytholm Bridge Viaduct.

When the line opened, the valley was crossed by a 26-bay timber trestle (like those seen in American 'wild west' movies), which spanned the New Mill Dyke. The trestle had a curved deck on a 20-chain radius, and this was needed so that the line could run on a ledge cut into the escarpment on the southern side of the Holme Valley and was essential if the line was to maintain the altitude required for the proposed extension on towards Holme Moss. The line actually fell on a gradient of 1 in 100 as far as Thongsbridge, but a climb of 1 in 120 on the subsequent 3/4-mile journey up to Holmfirth took the line to a terminus of 518 feet (158 metres) above sea level.

The deep valley carved by the New Mill Dyke presented a major problem for the railway and on account of the width of land needed to form the base for an embankment, plans for such a crossing were discounted in favour of the timber trestle. However, during the course of construction the spidery edifice was struck by strong winds and blown down. Local folk petitioned for its replacement to be built from stone, but when it was announced that the second structure would also be of timber there was considerable public concern. Fears continued after it was built, and despite a report from the great Robert Stephenson confirming its sound nature, public concerns continued until the L&YR eventually agreed to its replacement by a stone viaduct. Whilst work on this progressed, the wooden trestle remained in place, but was reduced to a single track line, to allow the other line to be used for the contractor's cranes and dereks. The inner line was then dismantled as each section of the new stone-built viaduct was completed, and long beams of Canadian Yellow Pine were employed to 'temporarily bolt the two sections together.'

Right: *Railway books often allude to the fact that signalmen often kept neat gardens around their 'boxes, but this series of pictures illustrate that the signal box at Brockholes was better tended than most. The top view shows the signage that Harold Armitage erected to commemorate the Queen's Coronation in 1952. The middle shot shows how the outside of the 'box was decked out with flowers and white-painted stones as borders, but the bottom view shows just how attractive the garden was. Again white-painted stones and well-tended flowers abound, but look at the small fish pond in the centre of the garden. This pool came complete with several goldfish that were tended by the signalman, despite the fact that this was alongside what was then a very busy main line. Harold Armitage*

Top Left: *As stated earlier, Brockholes was the centre of much railway activity, and prior to the merger of the L&YR and The London & North Western Railway in January 1922 it handled all the day to day management of the Huddersfield & Sheffield Junction Railway and the associated branches to Holmfirth, Meltham and Clayton West. As a 'District Yard' it had a staff out of all proportion to its size and rural location, although this was progressively reduced in number during LMS days. Francis Bray recalls that his two uncles were both relocated to Hillhouse at Huddersfield in 1925, and his father was moved to Penistone in 1948 when BR took charge. However, even into BR days the station had a substantial staff, and this view from 1957, shows the Brockholes Porter Geoff Quinn.*
Harold Armitage

Bottom Left: *Also captured by Harold Armitage, the tranquillity of a warm, sunny day outside the Signalling & Telegraph Store at Brockholes Junction, with (from left to right Geoff Quinn with Ronnie Mellor)*
Harold Armitage

On 1st November 1865 cracks were noticed in the seventh pier and buttresses were rapidly erected to support it. However on 3rd December 1865 the bad luck that had dogged the entire H&SJR line and branches was to rear its ugly head again, for as the work neared completion the 90-ft high viaduct collapsed, taking with it the timber trestle. The sound of the arches "going clap, clap, clap against one another" awoke William England the local corn miller, who watched as they tumbled down and filled the whole valley with dust. He dressed quickly and ran to the station to warn Stationmaster Haigh, as he knew a Holmfirth train was due to leave Huddersfield at 7am. Fortunately he managed to awaken the Stationmaster, who in turn told the signalman to stop the train from going along the branch. Oddly the signalman had not been alerted to the fact, as he was still in communication with Holmfirth and Thongsbridge, because the telegraph wires were still strung across the gap, even though the bridge had fallen.

An inquest into the collapse was held at Huddersfield in January 1866, when Captain Tyler for the Board of Trade announced that the collapse had occurred due to inadequacies in the construction work by the contractors, Henry Wadsworth & Co. They had built the No.7 pier partly on rock and partly on gravel, and due to improper supervision, this had not been noticed. The pier then slipped and fell. He also stated that "the person responsible for the task was insufficiently remunerated" and he further criticised "the niggardly manner of carrying on the work and the quality of the materials."

At this time the L&YR were heavily committed with work on the nearby Meltham Branch, and the company's engineer Sturgess Meek had taken up residence in Honley just one station back down the line. His first action was to clear up the mess and release the dam caused by debris holding back the New Mill Dyke, which he achieved by quickly sending a trainload of navvies diverted from work on the neighbouring branch. The next problem was how the services could be resumed whilst a replacement viaduct was erected.

As four carriages were left isolated at Holmfirth, consideration was given to taking a locomotive to the branch by road. However such an arrangement was clearly impractical, so 12 days later Meek entered into a contract with the Manchester Carriage Co., to provide a temporary 20-seater horse-bus service between Holmfirth, Honley and Brockholes.

The cost of the service was £1 for each return journey, on top of which the L&YR had to provide a conductor and pay the turnpike tolls. These tolls were eventually circumvented by the L&YR contriving to carry a mailbag on each journey, thus becoming exempt. Meek considered that the problems at Mytholm Bridge would be best resolved by reverting to the idea of constructing an embankment, which was particularly appealing in view of the huge quantities of spoil emanating from the Meltham branch construction sites which required disposal.

However, obtaining the required land turned out to be another matter, and in the end it was decided to re-build the viaduct and the contract was awarded to Gilbert & Sharp of Salford for £9,000. Despite the atrocious winter of 1866-7 the line re-opened to traffic ahead of schedule on 11th March 1867, earning the contractors a bonus of £400. Even then the winter was not over for the 200 or more people who had gathered to celebrate the arrival of the 'first' train at Holmfirth, as it pulled into the terminus in the midst of a violent snowstorm.

The stone viaduct was however a much more substantial structure than its predecessor and it would last until October 1976, when the British Railways Board decided it was cheaper to demolish the structure than keep up its maintenance. The contract was let to a local company, Bamforth's, but they had to make two attempts to demolish it with explosive charges. When the viaduct finally collapsed, it had not finished playing tricks on the people of the New Mill valley. Like the first 'fall' it managed to block the New Mill Dyke, although this was quickly resolved, but the blockage of the footpath along the valley floor took a little longer to put right. Even down to this day, substantial pieces of stone litter the valley floor, whilst the abutments clearly show where the problematical viaduct once stood.

Top Right: *The one thing that has emerged from my research into the Holmfirth branch line is the fact that this was a community within a community. Talking with people like Harold Armitage, Francis Bray, Gordon Ellis, Alvin Iredale, Percy Shaw and Brian Stott, it is clear that although they served at other railway locations, Holmfirth was always something special to them. Here we see two members of the Brockholes Junction staff, again with Geoff Quinn and Doug Hornsby, complete with a very smart-looking racing bike, on the right.* Harold Armitage

Bottom Right: *Though fog is obviously no cause for concern on the day this picture was taken at the junction, we see Jack Schofield a member of the Permanent Way Gang in the fog signalman's hut. Pictures of everyday railway operations such as fog signalling were rarely taken, and are even more rarely shown in railway books. Note the 'fire devil' stove alongside the signalman's hut, which appears to have been constructed from an old oil drum and a length of pipe.* Harold Armitage

THONGSBRIDGE STATION

South of the viaduct the branch entered a cutting which was spanned at either end by over-line road bridges, in between which was the site of Thongsbridge Station. Anonymous for most of its life, the station was a hive of activity and served the locality well for many years.

Above: *Passenger services from Thongsbridge to all stations for Huddersfield were always well patronised, but fewer people tended to use them on the short trip towards Holmfirth. In June 1959, 42189 leaves the station en-route to Leeds. It will be seen that the station canopy on the Up (Huddersfield-bound) platform has been removed by this stage, but we have not discovered a date when this work was done.* Peter Sunderland

Top Right: *This view, taken from the platform looks back to Heys Road bridge, and clearly shows the station buildings on the 'original' platform. On the right, the 'new' platform with its small waiting room was used by trains heading for Holmfirth. The two-storey booking office and the stone steps leading up to the road can be seen at the far end of the Up platform.*

Bottom Right: *This view taken in October 1954 looks north towards Springwood Road bridge. Seated on the bench are the incumbent porter and the Holmfirth booking clerk (who also had responsibility for the intermediate station). Comparing these pictures will show that this platform used at least three different types of station lamp over the years. The attractive gardens show that the staff had quite a bit of spare time on their hands.* Gordon Ellis

The original layout was somewhat different to how most people will recall. The maps on pages 34 show the original layout for the station, with its cramped location in the cutting between the bridges carrying Spring Wood Road and Heys Road. As a result of this, the Stationmaster's house and railway worker's cottage were located some distance from the station off Spring Wood Road. A long flight of steps connected the Huddersfield-bound platform up to Heys Road.

For many years a little newsagents shop was located opposite the station entrance, where the steps came up from the platform on to Heys Road. This shop was originally run by Fred Dyson, and when he retired was taken over by Colin and Sylvia Battye. In later years Colin purchased the former station site and generously presented the sandstone platform edging to the Keighley & Worth Valley Railway Preservation Society.

Above: *This view from the 1890s shows that the main station buildings at Thongsbridge were located on the Huddersfield-bound platform, whilst Holmfirth-bound passengers had a much more basic platform on the opposite side of the bridge. By the time the improvements were made, the Stationmaster was George T. Noble, but whether this view shows him or his predecessor, we cannot be certain. The view may well be connected with the pending improvements, as it shows all the station staff.* Alvin Iredale

When the line was originally constructed the two platforms were staggered on either side of the Heys Road over-line bridge at the west end of the cutting. As a result of safety concerns, a signal box was installed for the L&YR by the Gloucester Wagon Co. in 1880 just beyond the west end of the platform. A barrow crossing appears to have been the principal means of access to the Holmfirth-platform, but there may also have been a set of steps connecting it up onto the bridge.

Whatever the case, the platform arrangement was not only found to be difficult to operate, but it was twice seriously criticised by the Board of Trade; once after a very serious accident to a passenger using the barrow crossing, the other after a shunting accident in which a railway employee was injured.

As freight operations in the cramped goods yard (off Miry Lane) were also found to be very unsatisfactory, the L&YR outlined plans to re-build the station and widen the cutting in order to accommodate two platforms facing each other.

The contract for the improvement work was let to Robert Leake & Co. in 1893, as was another tender to extend the gap between the running lines from 5ft 9in to the more acceptable and standard 6-foot. The new two-storey booking office had mock Tudor framing on the upper section, from where an iron-lattice footbridge led to the new platform.

Top Right: *The improvements of 1901 saw a further siding being provided across the coal cells, whilst on the opposite side of the running lines another small yard was constructed. This was comprised of a long trailing siding from which a further siding diverged. As the yard was now on both sides of the running lines, a cartway provided access between the two sides and a lifting barrier, constructed from standard signalling parts, protected the crossing.*

Bottom Right: *The signal box at Thongsbridge with Brian Stott looking out. Brian recalls one of the regular sources of outward traffic as being wool rugs made at local mills like Boothroyds and Hobsons.* Both Brian Stott

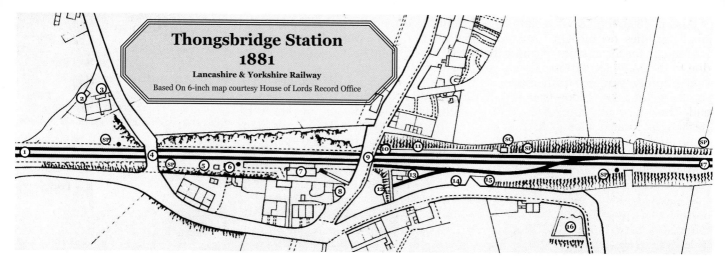

MAP OF 1881

SC	Signal Cabin	10	Barrow crossing
SP	Signal Post	11	Down Platform
1	To Huddersfield	12	Merchant's Office
2	Stationmaster's House	13	Goods office & Weigh-house
3	Railway Cottage	14	Hand Crane
4	Springwood Rd. Bridge	15	Coal Staithes
5	Permanent Way Store	16	Reservoir
6	Porter's room	17	To Holmfirth
7	Waiting rooms/offices		
8	Foot steps to platform		
9	Heys Road Bridge		

MAP OF 1931

SC	Signal Cabin	SP	Signal Post
1	To Huddersfield	12	Booking Hall
2	Stationmaster's House	13	Heys Road Bridge
3	Railway Cottage	14	Weighbridge & Office
4	Wooldale Co-op Coal	15	Dyson's coal office
5	Springwood Rd. Bridge	16	Armitage's coal office
6	Permanent Way Store	17	Hand Crane
7	Lamp room	18	Gated sleeper crossing
8	Down Waiting Room	19	Coal Drops
9	Footbridge	20	Down Sidings
10	Up Waiting Room	21	Mound
11	Footsteps to platform	22	Old Reservoir
		23	To Holmfirth

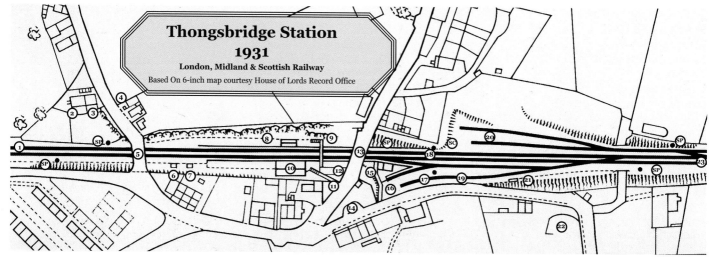

Also in 1893, the L&YR took the opportunity to extend the goods yard, as the small facilities on the Up (or Huddersfield-bound) line were by then totally inadequate for the amount of traffic that was by then being handled. Additionally, due to the way Holmfirth coal yard was then being worked, it was necessary to stable empty wagons further back down the line. The initial facilities were comprised of a single loop from which a small siding was thrown at the southern end. Three new coal drops were created under the loop, whilst a three-ton yard crane was located alongside the short siding. The additional facilities were comprised of an extra siding on the Up line and two sidings on the Down line.

When the old Down platform was removed and re-located into the cutting opposite the Up platform, a wooden 'cartway' was provided so that road vehicles could cross from the original goods yard to the new facility on the opposite side of the tracks. However, the Board of Trade refused to sanction the use of this crossing at first, as no means of mechanical protection had been installed to protect either the road or the rail users. The L&YR rapidly addressed this omission and built an 'interlocked level crossing', which was simply a pair of barriers linked to the signal cabin by standard signalling parts. I recall standing on the bridge carrying Heys Road on the last afternoon's operation in the Spring of 1965, watching this barrier system being raised after the very last train steamed off back towards Huddersfield. Sadly I had no camera to hand to record its final use, and as schoolboys we never really gave much thought to the recording of a passing era; what a wonderful thing hindsight is!

In the years before closure, Thongsbridge was a busy little goods yard, which saw a lot of traffic despite its proximity to Holmfirth. Unusual deliveries came in the form of Argentinian guano and American sulphate, which were received for Batley's size, bone and manure (fertiliser) works just below the station off Miry Lane. Another kind of inward traffic was seen with the receipt of lengths of timber that were turned into bobbins by the Lockwood family who used part of Mytholm Bridge Mill for their Moorland Wood Turning Company. Yet it was with carriage of coal traffic, that the yard was mainly occupied.

The Wooldale Co-operative Society had an office and weighbridge on Springwood Road and some of the men who ran this office are recalled as being Charlie Lockwood (1915-45), Eric Dearnley (1946-52), Ronnie Ellis (1952-7) and Maurice Scott (1957 to closure). Another Ellis family were the three brothers from Scholes who had a haulage business employing Bedford lorries to take coal up to the area around Scholes (including the co-operative society). In addition to this, the co-ops at Netherthong and Hepworth also had coal delivered to the yard. However, the climb up to Netherthong was exceptionally steep, so the co-op wagons had to be given an extra horse to enable them to reach the hilltop village.

Armitage's coal merchants and Fred Dyson both had offices in the yard, whilst the weighbridge was alongside Miry Lane; its incumbent for many years being Allen Morton. Robinson's dye-works also used horse wagons to collect their coal, as did Woodhead's, who continued to do so well into the era of motor lorries as the passage leading to their Albion Mills boiler house was so narrow. In later years I recall that the horse was replaced by a trailer drawn by a little grey Ferguson tractor. The same tractor also collected bales of raw wool from the goods yard.

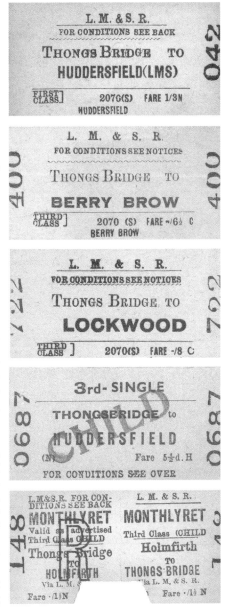

Above: *A selection of branch line tickets from the collection of Gordon Ellis. Gordon recalls that some LMS tickets were still being used in 1959.*

Above: *Thousands of tons of coal must have been handled at Thongsbridge over the years, most of it shovelled from the wagons or coal cells by hand. Here John Bailes is pictured with coal wagons and a delivery lorry on the siding at the Down (Holmfirth-bound) side of the yard.* Brian Stott

As an example of the textile traffic we might mention the two nearest mills, which were located at the bottom of Miry Lane. These were Thongs Bridge Mill and Albion Mill, both of which were located just below the station and alongside the River Holme.

These two mills took large quantities of 'steam' coal as well as wool from Bradford, Halifax and Huddersfield. In turn they despatched finished pieces of cloth as outward traffic. In later years, as the industry went into decline, many local mills closed down; even so, some continued to use rail transport. One such instance was Ford Mills between Scholes and Wooldale, which had been started as a yarn spinning mill, at Shaley Wood in 1862 by Alfred Wood. It later became the firm of Wood & Burtt, but in 1919 was purchased by J. & J. Baldwin of Halifax. Following a merger, this became Paton & Baldwin, who in the mid-1950s ceased production at Ford Mill and used it for warehousing. For several years the yarn was collected by British Railways lorries and taken to Thongsbridge for despatch by rail.

When I began researching my books *British Railways Road Vehicles 1948-1968* and *LMS Railway Road Vehicles*, I found (much to my surprise) a great deal of mention about the road cartage at Holmfirth and Thongsbridge. Ultimately I managed to make contact with Alvin Iredale of Glossop, who had been one of the Cartage Department drivers. He began at Huddersfield (Fitzwilliam Street Depot) on coming out of the army in 1946, and was then issued with a 'civvy license' on account of his military driving experience.

After 16-months on town cartage, he was allocated to the Holmfirth out-station, and used a Mechanical Horse for six or seven months. This was of 1934 vintage, and was notable for gearbox troubles. In early-1948 he was given a 2-ton Austin drop-side with a half-canvas tilt, which was sometimes kept in the open at Thongsbridge. However, with the change of railway timetables and starting times making for a long cycle ride from his 'digs' in Fartown, he managed to get lodgings with a local railwayman and his family for seven shillings and sixpence a week.

His early-turn duties involved "taking parcels from the early trains to local business premises, and fresh fish to local chip shops." Most of his delivery work was based out of Thongsbridge, but his collection work all went back to Holmfirth. Two other out-station vehicles were allocated to the Holme Valley, a 30-cwt Morris Commercial 'Express Parcels' van and a 15-cwt Karrier van; both of which were kept at the Holmfirth Garage but were sometimes stabled at Thongsbridge. However, "after the North Eastern Region was formed in 1956 all the vehicles were 'recalled' to Huddersfield, and thereafter worked from there."

This page: *These two views show the type of railway road vehicles employed in the Holme Valley. The top view shows a Fordson B type van, LMS fleet no. 333, the sister of which (329) was based at the Holmfirth Motor Transport Department Garage in the 1930s. The lower one is a Scammell Townsman at Huddersfield, which often worked up to Holmfirth by road after the branch closed. Unfortunately BR's national road collection and delivery service, as a whole, was considered to be grossly unprofitable. In 1955/6 the Holme Valley road motor service was centralised on Holmfirth, but after the garage there closed in (or around) 1957/8 it was then operated from Huddersfield. This caused numerous delays, and firms like Paton & Baldwin soon realised it was cheaper to employ their own road vehicles.*

Above: *The goods yard at Thongsbridge was originally operated by a lever-worked from the signal box and inter-locked with signals for the running lines, but this installation took up all the spare capacity of the original frame. Accordingly, this was replaced with an L&YR 24-lever frame in 1909, which lasted until the line was singled on 10th-11th June 1961, allowing the closure of the box. The goods yard arrangement is seen here in June 1959, as 42189 heads through with a*

Holmfirth - Huddersfield - Leeds (New Line) stopping train. The goods yard looks exceptionally busy with a mixture of coal wagons, general merchandise trucks and a couple of box vans; one of which is of Southern Railway origin. Although the coal drops are obscured by the smoke from the Fairburn 2-6-4T, the paved cartway and the sleeper crossing are clearly visible. Note the lifting barrier that protects the running lines.
Peter Sunderland

At the west end of the goods yard an under-line bridge was crossed, before the branch passed along a short embankment followed by an over-line bridge carrying Berry Bank Lane (the original main road from Huddersfield to Woodhead). A short cutting followed, but this soon gave way on the northern side as the land began to fall away towards the River Holme. At this point a plate-layers cabin was found on the eastern side of the line. With a cutting face on the south-western side of the line it continued towards Berry Banks outside Holmfirth. This was an exceptionally pretty stretch of the line, but your author has less pleasant memories of the Berry Banks however, after losing a large portion of muscle from his upper arm when attacked by a bull-mastiff alongside the railway in October 1963.

Shortly after Berry Banks the head-shunt of Holmfirth Goods Yard was reached. This ran alongside the Huddersfield-bound line, but in the early days it had no connection to the running tracks. This was rectified by the improvements of the 1890s that provided a cross-over to release trains from the goods yard, but as there was no connection to the Up line this still meant that incoming freight trains still had to draw into the platform road before shunting could begin.

Top Right: *When I began taking photos in the early 1960s, I thought it might be a good idea to record the general scene. As a result August 1963 saw this view being taken of the platelayers' hut near Berry Banks.*

Bottom Right: *In the Spring of 1964, there were three visits by an engineer's inspection saloon. The first, on 2nd April was behind B1 class 4-6-0 (61021 Reitbok) whilst that on the 20th was with a Jubilee class 4-6-0 (45626 Seychelles); the other working (seen whilst we were doing a school cross-country run) was in the care of an un-named Black Five. All three of these were connected with the final demise of the line, which had been singled three years earlier. Here we see the station throat in 1962, a year after that work had been done! Quite when the final lifting took place is not properly recorded, and various dates have been quoted to me in 1965 and 1966.*

HOLMFIRTH STATION

Holmfirth was an unusual terminus, as (for a number of years) it featured a turntable at the western end of the platform. This 45-foot (13.75-metre) diameter locomotive turntable was installed by the L&YR in March 1883 as a prelude to the various station improvements that were to follow. The station therefore has inspired a number of model layouts, including one that I built and was featured in the *Railway Modeller* magazine in 1989.

Above: *In a view dating from June 1959, Ivatt 2-6-2T, 41258 has just arrived from Bradford with a four-coach train The view shows the site of the Piece Warehouse (demolished in 1956 and evidenced by the clean stonework) and the fact that the platform canopy has also been cut back for quite some length. In the distance you can see the signal box, whilst on the right is the goods warehouse. The signal box was a timber-built 'box with a 24-lever Gloucester Wagon Co. frame that was erected for the L&YR in 1882 on the probable site of the old water tower.*
J. Davenport

Strangely, the turntable did not replace the 'cross-over' at the west-end of the platform, as the point-work was retained with its 'toe end' butting onto the turntable well. This point was not connected to the signal box but worked by a single-lever Railway Signal Co. frame located at the bottom of the platform ramp. Behind this ramp stood an old lamp hut and oil store, which was in fact the remains of an L&YR three-compartment coach.

The story goes the coach had run away one night, and after falling into the turntable pit was found to be too badly damaged to be repaired. Accordingly its body was hauled out and pressed into use in place of another hut, which stood nearer to the buffers. Investigation of this building in 1968 revealed that beneath the tongue and groove outer cladding, it was indeed a four-wheeled coach body that had suffered some severe damage. When measured it was apparent from the dimensions that half of one compartment was completely missing.

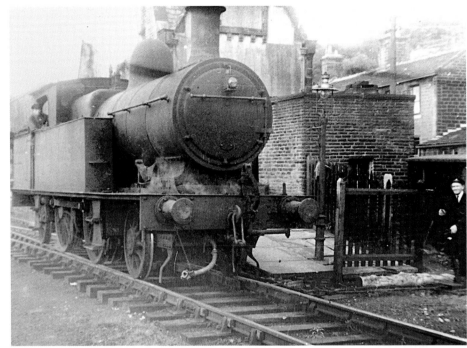

Top Right: *Just a few weeks after Nationalisation in January 1948, an unidentified Aspinall 2-4-2T comes off its four-coach passenger train to run round Devoid of its smokebox number plate, the locomotive will cross the toe of the points, before the porter-signalman on the right (Herbert Jessop) throws the ground frame lever to change the 'road'.*

Bottom Right: *The lamp hut at the station was the body of an old four-wheeled carriage. By 1962 the area around the platform end has become unkempt, and the remains of a child's swing dangles pathetically from the ladder arm of the gas lamp.*

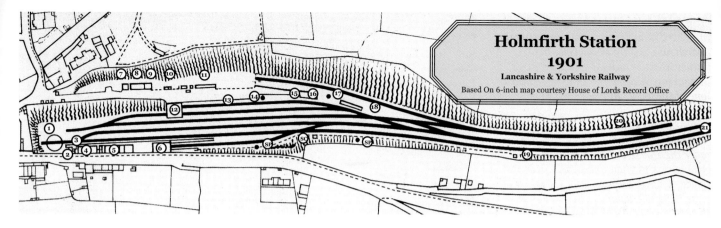

Holmfirth Station
1901
Lancashire & Yorkshire Railway
Based On 6-inch map courtesy House of Lords Record Office

MAP OF 1901		MAP OF 1941	
SC Signal Cabin	11 Merchant's offices	SC Signal Cabin	11 Merchant's offices
SP Signal Post	12 General Warehouse	SP Signal Post	12 General Warehouse
1 Turntable	13 Coal Drops	1 Oil store	13 Coal Drops
2 Lamp hut (old coach)	14 Hand Crane	2 Lamp hut (old coach)	14 Hand Crane
3 Groundframe	15 Low-level timber stage	3 Groundframe	15 Low-level timber stage
4 Stationmaster's House	16 Cattle Dock	4 Stationmaster's House	16 Cattle Dock
5 Waiting rooms & Booking Office	17 Hand Crane	5 Waiting rooms & Booking Office	17 Hand Crane
6 Piece Goods Warehouse	18 Gas Company Office	6 Piece Goods Warehouse	18 Goods Office
7 Cartage Office	19 Permanent Way Hut	7 Goods Office	19 Permanent Way Hut
8 Stables	20 Ground Frame	8 Garage	20 Ground Frame
9 Tack/harness room	21 To Huddersfield	9 Petrol store	21 To Huddersfield
10 Weigh-house		10 Weigh-house	

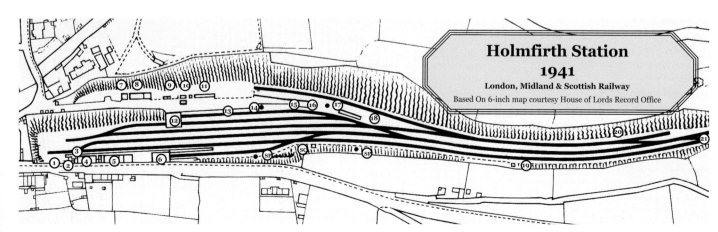

Holmfirth Station
1941
London, Midland & Scottish Railway
Based On 6-inch map courtesy House of Lords Record Office

Top Right: *Looking from the platform, it is hard to appreciate that the general warehouse was on two levels. It measured approximately 50-feet in length and 30-feet in width. It spanned one of the loop sidings, and was unusual in the fact that it was served by one of the roads over the coal drops. As locomotives were not permitted to pass over the wooden deck of the coal drops, trucks or vans had to be propelled into place at the end of a rake of trucks. It was therefore common, in mixed goods trains, for the general merchandise vehicles to be marshalled at the front; this marshalling being done at either Mirfield or Lockwood goods yards (at least in L&YR days). Once the vehicles had been dealt with in the goods shed, a locomotive could draw out up to two vehicles at a time from the southern end. Inside the shed a hand-operated 3-ton jib crane was located.*

Bottom Right: *Viewed from the opposite side, the general warehouse was pictured in 1963. The door at the northern end was originally fitted with a 'man access door', but following a shunting accident in the late-1949 or early-1950 the door was destroyed and an access door was not incorporated in the replacement. Alvin Iredale recalls the incident, as he was waiting at the yard with his Austin 2-ton lorry, he said "we had a fairly long train of vans behind an Austerity 2-8-0 from Sheffield. It was an unusual working, and had a driver from Millhouses, but he had a Hillhouse man with him as a 'pilot'. They came in on the platform road, ran around the train and pulled it back into the sidings; however when they went forward again, somebody had a mix-up and the leading van was pushed straight through the shed door."*

Top Left: *This exterior view of the station was taken in the early 1950s, when the station was declaring a mixed identity. The name L&YR still appears carved in stone above the entry doors.* A.H.A. Bastable

Bottom Left: *This view was taken 40 years later, following the refurbishment of the Stationmaster's house and the demolition of the 'new' booking office. The station had become very derelict by the late 1970s, but on 1st June 1979, the* Huddersfield Examiner *carried a feature, stating that the whole site was on sale at just £15,000.*

Gordon Ellis, who trained as a booking clerk at Holmfirth in 1954, recalls what the station was like just over a century on from its opening:-

"At this time the staff comprised of the Stationmaster, booking clerk and (I think) two porters, one for the early turn and the other the late, plus a goods clerk. The Stationmaster was a rather shadowy figure who did not seem to venture far from his office and when he did his dog usually followed him. I got the impression that so long as things were running smoothly that he left well alone.

Parcels traffic was still reasonably busy, and those that had arrived on the morning trains had to be delivered. Delivery sheets had to be prepared and then the porter helped the van driver to load them. On occasions baskets of racing pigeons arrived. These had to be released from the platform at the precise time given on the basket – one of the highlights of the day!

Goods were still frequently sent by passenger train and people would often arrive with parcels of all kinds. The railway was still a 'common carrier' and almost anything could be sent. We dealt with boxes of day old chicks, boxes of books, unaccompanied bicycles, and cases containing an array of goods.

On one occasion a young live calf, neatly wrapped in sacking, was brought in for despatch. Fortunately it only had to go to a farm on the other side of Leeds!

The most hectic part of the day was always between 16.30 when the van driver came back from his rounds, and the departure of the tea-time train at about 17.15. The delivery driver usually arrived with parcels of postcards from Bamforths, cloth pieces from the local mills, iron castings from Longbottoms and various others. Apart from the dead weight of the postcards the main problem was with the castings. It was not unusual for these items to have been made that morning, and then painted in the afternoon. The paint was rarely properly dry! It was hard work to lift them on to the scales and attach a transit slip without getting paint everywhere. All this would be going on whilst the train was in the station with the departure time fast approaching.

All outgoing items had to be entered into an appropriate ledger and in quiet times it made fascinating reading to see what had been sent in times past. The thing that stands out vividly in my mind were the entries of the despatch of coffins complete with the deceased, about five or six as I recall. These occurred during the war and were, I was told, the remains of evacuees being returned to their homes. No charge was made for this service."

Top Right: *Standing beside the former piece warehouse, 41258 basks in the sun. The warehouse was a two-storey affair, with road access being obtained onto the upper floor from the New Mill road. The pieces were then dropped (through hatches in the floor) into the waiting wagons or roof-door vans below*

Bottom Right: *From the 'clean' stonework the site of the old Piece Warehouse is quite obvious in this 1962 picture.*

Passenger Services

The line was always well patronised and for many years there was no competing bus service, so passenger trains regularly consisted of three or more carriages, but at the very start the railway did not have the most auspicious beginnings. The dual operation of the branch by the L&YR and the MS&LR in 1850 does not appear to have worked out for the benefit of the passengers, and it would seem that little effort was made to guarantee connections.

Above: *The provision of the turntable was the first stage in a variety of improvements during the latter part of the 19th century. This enabled the turning of locomotives, so the L&YR practice of working smokebox out, bunker back was stopped, even though engines such as the Aspinall 2-4-2 Radial Tank were quite adept at this form of operation. Indeed, up to the disaster at Charleston Curve in the Calder Valley on 21st June 1912, the L&YR used such engines as express locomotives. Here (10822) a long-bunkered member of the class is seen at right-angles to the running line in LMS days.*

Right: *In 1890 the goods office was transferred into one of the new buildings on the goods yard approach road, roughly opposite the lower-ground floor of the warehouse. Thereafter the old goods office, which had been part of the large Stationmaster's house at the southern end of the platform, was taken over by the incumbent as his office. Around this time the platforms were also extended to accommodate the longer trains now using the station, but there was a noticeable difference in the height of the two sections. By the mid-1890s, with plans for an extension finally abandoned, a series of major improvements were ordered by the L&YR. Contract drawings for platform improvements were prepared by J. Chadwick & Son in October 1896, and work commenced about 11 weeks later. The original platform's height was raised to match the newer section and it was extended along as far as the turntable well. The bay platform was filled in between the new waiting rooms and booking office and the Piece Warehouse. What remained in 1962 is pictured here.*

The worst train service in the early years was the 3.32pm departure from Penistone, which missed the connection to Huddersfield and Bradford at Brockholes by a matter of minutes and passengers were faced with a three-and-a-half hour wait for the next service. Yet this departure from Penistone was the one that connected with the express from Sheffield to Manchester, which was one of the MS&LR's best-used services. It took just 36 minutes to reach Penistone from Sheffield as opposed to the 46 or 49 minutes of all the other services, yet once the passengers changed on to the H&SJR it would take them over four hours to reach Huddersfield.

Above: *Many stations were often located some distance from the community they were supposed to serve (Honley is a good example) but Holmfirth's was just a few minutes walk to the town centre. This view of 41258 gives a good impression of both the station and the town. Note the proximity of the gas works to the station; its site was carefully chosen to allow the easy carriage of coal from the coal cells on the right.* J. Davenport

The quickest run from Sheffield to Huddersfield was the 10.01am that took 104 minutes, whilst the most useful departure from Sheffield, the 5.45pm took 141 minutes. Southbound the first journey offering a connection to Sheffield was the 6.58am from Huddersfield that took two hours 38 minutes, whilst two other workings both took three hours 38 minutes.

If the timetabling was bad, adherence to it was even worse. On the first Market Day, Tuesday 2nd July 1850, over 969 tickets were sold from Holmfirth alone. When this is coupled with receipts from other stations on the H&SJR (excluding Huddersfield itself) 1,437 market-return tickets were sold. The company totally under-estimated the demand on the service and when the return train arrived from Bradford (one hour late) it was already terribly over-crowded.

Many passengers decided to walk home, others crowded into the 18 extra coaches that were added at Huddersfield. Even the resulting 38-coach train was incapable of carrying all who wanted to travel, and an extra train had to be put on at 7.15pm. Three weeks later an article in the *Huddersfield Chronicle*, reprinted in facsimile below, read:

FURTHER ANNOYANCES ON THE HUDDERSFIELD & PENISTONE RAILWAY

We have during the past two weeks been called upon most reluctantly to complain on the manner in which the passengers on this line are being accommodated, but as yet we regret that no improvements have been made, nor any steps to remedy the gross mis-management which has characterized the working of this railway since it first opened.

The article then went on to quote the case of a trader (travelling salesman) who had caught the 10.01am train from Sheffield to Manchester as it was supposed to connect with the service to Huddersfield at Penistone, but when it got in (on time) the service for Huddersfield had already left and was passing them en-route for the junction. He was thus forced to wait with about 40 other passengers until the 3.32pm service, which perversely left at 4.00pm. It was promised that a connection would be made at Holmfirth Junction with an extra train from Holmfirth, but when they arrived there the passengers were told to get out of the train and prepare for a 'long wait' as the next train would not leave until 6.40pm.

The traveller decided enough was enough and started to walk to Huddersfield. He arrived there at 6pm, but his fellow travellers who had waited at Brockholes did not arrive in the town until 7pm, their journey had taken nine hours. The newspaper concluded "If the railway company fancy that the general public will much longer submit to such mismanagement we suspect the sequel will show them that they are reckoning without their host!"

It may be easy to dismiss this atrocious situation as teething troubles, but the facts show a much deeper problem with locomotive shortages being the crux of the matter. More letters of complaint were written to the press on 27th July (Berry Brow trains running from 30 minutes to one hour late), 17th August (Holmfirth trains leaving the branch early) and 24th August (passengers from Bradford to Holmfirth being turned off the train at Huddersfield whilst the engine and carriages proceeded on quite empty).

However, the L&YR were managing to get some things right and on 11th August the Huddersfield Oddfellows Friendly Society organised a Sunday picnic excursion to Holmfirth. With the price being equal to one third of the normal return fare, the 205 members of the Society were joined by a further 2,135 'friends' who wanted tickets.

As the railway could not accommodate such a large number, the L&YR put forward a compromise that would see one train of 36 coaches making two journeys to Holmfirth at 9.30am and 10.45am respectively. Being the Sabbath a service was arranged in Holmfirth with a local Methodist minister presiding at an open-air service, after which the visitors wandered around the town and nearby moors.

The day passed off without incident, but the same could not be said for a special that left the branch for Huddersfield on 1st October in connection with a concert at the Huddersfield Philharmonic Hall. The outward journey was without incident as extra coaches were put on the scheduled evening passenger trains that ran at 3.20pm, 6.30pm and 7.50pm.

The return was to be by means of a special train but when the concert-goers arrived back at the station, they found that the L&YR had failed to provide an engine, and what was more, when officials were questioned the travellers were told "the company had no intention of finding one at such a late hour." The affluent managed to find a cab, but the vast majority were forced to walk back to Holmfirth or Brockholes.

This act earned the L&YR an even worse reputation than before, but it also led them before the law courts when 15 passengers sued for 'Breach of Contract'. As a result, the L&YR were forced to compensate the claimants for the cost of their cab fares. The magistrates also decided that the L&YR should be penalised much harder and made an award of 10s 6d (52.5p) for each passenger who could prove that they had been inconvenienced by the non-arrival of the advertised service; in total 432 passengers were so compensated.

As the autumn progressed and winter set in, the problems deteriorated even more as the difficulties caused by locomotive shortages worsened. Trains on both the main line and the branch were frequently cancelled by the L&YR, whilst the MS&LR appeared to become completely indifferent about the service it was supposed to be offering to Holmfirth.

Of the trains that ran, little attention was given to the connections at Penistone and Holmfirth Junction. The attacks on the railway became even more vitriolic and the press in Huddersfield, Bradford and Sheffield all carried articles and letters about the poor service. Train operations did improve as the New Year arrived, but an article in the *Leeds Mercury* in 1852 showed that things were still no better over connections when it reported "it was about time that the L&YR took over those trains in which the MS&L are conveying passengers to Holmfirth Junction, and thereby provide a more commodious form of transport twixt Bradford and Sheffield." Despite this plea it seems as though the railway companies were quite content with the shared service arrangement, although there were "continued improvements being made all the while."

The shortage of trains and poor connections between the L&YR and MS&LR trains was serious enough, but most of the complaints were about missed services from Holmfirth. Though the railway service was undoubtedly poor, one under-lying reason for many of the problems resulted from the fact that the parish church clock was some 15 minutes slow. This fact appears to have escaped most people's attention until a letter appeared in the local paper pointing out the differences between ecclesiastical time and railway time.

Despite the problems occasioned by the MS&LR and L&YR's shared traffic arrangement, railway travel was capturing the attention of a large cross-section of the public and demand for special trains continued unabated.

At Honley Feast (September) 1851 a total of 1,190 people travelled on an excursion from the branch, whilst on the occasion of the tragic bursting of the Bilberry Reservoir in 1852 a special excursion of 362 ghoulish tourists came from Manchester to witness the effects of the tidal wave that devastated the Holme Valley. The Sunday evening excursions from Holmfirth to Penistone were also very popular, and on one occasion over 3,000 people were carried in one evening - it is not surprising to read that all the pubs in the town ran dry!

Other early excursions are recorded to have gone to Liverpool, Manchester, Matlock and Hull. In the case of the latter excursion, Thomas Normington recorded in his book on the L&YR that his heavily loaded train had to be divided between Thongsbridge and Holmfirth on the return journey. Around midnight, whilst waiting for the engine to return from taking the front portion to the terminus, Normington says that he heard another train coming down the branch behind. So he took steps to warn its driver. Fortunately disaster was narrowly averted, and if Normington was not exaggerating, the second engine came to a stop just 12 inches from the rear of the stationary coaches.

Quite when the L&YR assumed the complete working of the branch is not known, but this was certainly by 1854, as it is said that the Penistone-facing curve at Holmfirth Junction (Brockholes) was removed in the October of that year. In 1860 there were eight passenger trains running in each direction on the branch, with several of these working through to Bradford or Halifax. By 1879 this had increased to nine trains each way, Monday to Friday, with an extra Saturday service, but only three return journeys on a Sunday.

The time taken by almost all the trains around this period was 23 minutes from Holmfirth and 25 minutes from Huddersfield, the only exception being the 2.48pm ex-Huddersfield (24 minutes) and the return 'Market Day Special' (9pm ex-Huddersfield) which (at 27 minutes) took the longest due to the heavy load it carried.

Actually, the cheap Market Day tickets (which were issued to Huddersfield and Halifax only) often resulted in extra coaches being added to the 12.40pm train. Trains were often so busy that ticket collectors boarded evening trains at Thongsbridge or Brockholes in order to relieve congestion at the Holmfirth ticket barrier when the train arrived.

Top Right: *In the late 1940s, BR-LMR provided facilities for the Matisa Company to test their tamping equipment on sections of the main line and on the Holmfirth branch. Seen at Berry Brow, this tamper had a Leyland diesel engine for propulsion and the air compressor which supplied air for the vertical reciprocation of the 16 tamping tools, while the vibratory and packing movements of the tamping tools were by means of chain drives.* Harold Armitage

Bottom Right: *Hughes Crab 2-6-0, 42719, heads past Berry Brow goods yard on Saturday 11th June 1949. This is a three-coach passenger train to Holmfirth, and is unusual as it boasts a tender engine. Although tender engines regularly worked the branch, the majority seem to have been camera shy.*
The late Frank Alcock

With the exception of the 'Market Day Special', none of the Holmfirth trains worked beyond Huddersfield after 1st August 1879. The reason for this is associated with the introduction of the Clayton West trains that became an integral part of the Holmfirth service between Huddersfield and Brockholes and vice-versa.

Around this time pressure on platform availability at Huddersfield meant there was no capacity for any more services, so 'slip working' of the Clayton West coaches was introduced. These were attached to the Holmfirth trains, but this led to several accidents at Brockholes. Once this operation was condemned the through working of Holmfirth trains began once more. Thereafter Halifax and Leeds were the most common destinations, although one early train from Mirfield was handled by a loco from Goole.

Above: *Taken sometime in the 1930s, this Aspinall 2-4-2 Radial Tank Engine is pictured in Wakefield Kirkgate Station with a mid-morning train to Goole. This working originated at Goole, leaving the inland port at 4.38am. It ran to Wakefield, conveying milk and newspapers, before forming the first train from Mirfield to Holmfirth. It returned with passengers to Huddersfield, and then ran ECS to Mirfield, whence it became the all-stations train to Goole.* Real Photos

One interesting working was the provision of through coaches to Blackpool that commenced in 1896, and were added to the trans-Pennine services at Halifax Station. Seasonal or regular trains to the Lancashire resort remained a feature into the Edwardian era, and the line was always busy. Even during World War I, when massive cuts in services were forced on the railways, Holmfirth managed to maintain a fairly intensive service.

Top Right: *Although this view is not on the Holmfirth Branch, it is representative of the kind of train that would have been operated on L&YR branch lines around the end of the 19th century. The locomotive is a Barton-Wright 0-4-4 tank engine (12) and the carriage is a six-wheeled L&YR coach with a guard's compartment and brake.*

Bottom Right: *This view is taken at Crewe Works in 1926, and shows an Aspinall 0-6-0 class 3F locomotive (12373). It was built in January 1898 and was allocated to Mirfield shed in the early 1900s as L&YR 609. It was a regular visitor to the Holmfirth branch, and Francis Bray recalls it was the first engine upon which he ever managed to beg a footplate ride.*

Initially, when the locomotive and staff shortages of 1917 resulted in massive cutbacks on Britain's railways everywhere, the branch saw the suspension of through trains to Huddersfield, the withdrawal of the last train of the day and the loss of all Sunday services. A tank locomotive was then used to operate a Holmfirth - Brockholes shuttle, but as traffic increased rather than declined, the L&YR were forced to re-introduce through trains. The *Holmfirth Express* remarked upon the event, saying it was "about time the railway authorities came to their senses!"

After the war, most railways began to feel the effect of road-vehicle competition, and Holmfirth was not immune. However, after an initial period of outright competition, the bus operators like Haigh Wilson, Green & White (later Baddeley Bros.) tended to offer services that fed the railway rather than competed with it.

Top Left: *This Leyland Cub with a Charles Roe (B20F) illustrates the motorbus development in the Holme Valley. Following the 1930 Road Traffic Act, the LMS began a joint undertaking with Huddersfield Corporation to form a Joint Omnibus Committee. It came into being on 16th May 1930 and in June 1934, it bought out the Holmfirth firm of Wilson Haigh.*

Bottom Left: *Long after both the railway and the HJOC succumbed, Baddeley Brothers continued to serve the people of the Holme and Don valleys. Here we see one of three new buses bought in 1953, No 49 (JWX 823) was a Commer Avenger with a full-front 32-seat Harrington body. Pictured here in Huddersfield on the Hepworth Iron Company workman's contract service, it also displays the firm's famous 'Land Cruiser' slogan. R. Mack courtesy Baddeley Brothers*

Right: *Pictures of the last train have sadly proved illusive, despite numerous appeals! So, as an illustration of what it was like in the final weeks, this picture of Fowler 2-6-4T (42413) in October 1959 is the best example of this period. Other Fowler side-window tanks known to have worked this line are 42406, 42408, 42409, 42410,42412, 42414, 42418 and 42419. Gavin Morrison*

A very large area of attractive countryside lies between Holmfirth and the Woodhead line to the south and the Meltham branch to the north, and it proved fertile territory for a number of the enterprising bus operators, especially for Sunday excursions from Huddersfield to the Pennine moors to the west of the town.

Despite bus competition and the effects of the General Strike and the Depression, Holmfirth did not suffer too great a reduction in traffic, and by the end of the 1920s business was back at pre-war levels. In 1926 the LMS, fearful of the growing competition from Baddeley Brothers' excursion business, re-introduced the Sunday service, and it was at once well patronised.

The year 1930 was particularly significant for the local transport scene, when Huddersfield Corporation entered into joint omnibus operation with the LMS. By purchasing half of the motorbus fleet the LMS gained an important share in local transport services, adding it to the railways, canals, and road haulage services that they already owned.

Even though bus competition significantly increased, passenger receipts did not drop dramatically, and there seems to have been greater integration between rail and road services. One significant loss however was the turntable that was taken out of service in the autumn of 1938, when it was found that its cross-members and bearings were badly in need of replacement.

Because the 2-4-2 and 2-6-4 tanks that then worked the bulk of the line's service could run in either direction, a replacement seemed superfluous. Thereafter the majority of LMS trains worked tender-first to Holmfirth, smokebox back, although this was not always the case as several people have told me.

Above: *Herbert Jessop (a porter at Holmfirth since 1922 - seen centre) arranged a photographic tribute to record the end of the passenger service. Stationmaster, Robert Tait (second from the right), said he could not remember an occasion like it, and estimated that he had sold about 100 tickets for the last train. The last passenger train signalman, Harold Armitage (on the right) kindly loaned this copy of the picture.*

The line still enjoyed a lavish daily passenger service, though this was savagely pruned at the outset of World War II when Sunday trains were withdrawn entirely. By the end of the 1950s, the passenger service had shrunk to just four trains each way (Monday to Saturday), although these were still well patronised. Despite the fact that most of the departures from Holmfirth now seemed suited to the railway's schedule, rather than being for the convenience of the passengers.

Evening trains were a thing of the past, and the remaining workings were hardly suited to workers or schoolchildren, whilst the 'shoppers' trains' were not convenient either." Nevertheless, the trains were reasonably patronised, and there was talk of dieselising the local passenger services in the Huddersfield area from 1959 onwards. Holmfirth still looked to have a reasonable future. It was even thought that evening trains could be re-introduced, whilst talk of better communications for school children were one of the desires of the County Council's Upper Agbrigg Education Executive.

In a re-shaping of schools in the Holme Valley, it had been decided to create two main centres of learning for children over the age of 11, and this offered some hope of a life-line for the branch. Grammar school education was to be provided in Honley, and the site (just a few hundred yards from the railway station) was to be developed.

Meanwhile, a 'green field' site was to be provided just above Thongsbridge Station for a new secondary modern school (later known as Holmfirth High School), the first stage of which would open in 1959. The concept behind the new schools provision was that the Holme Valley's educational needs could be taken as a whole. All the children who passed the 'Eleven-Plus' would thereafter be sent to the Honley Grammar School, and all others would be sent to the brand new Holmfirth Secondary Modern. The drawback to this arrangement would be the need for bussing pupils across the catchment area, and the most direct roads between Honley and Thongsbridge were unsuitable for the purpose. However, West Riding Council had identified the railway as being a much more convenient means of travel, and had asked BR to look at re-scheduling its timetable from September 1959.

Local coach operators, Baddeleys and G. W. Castle were asked to tender for the services to the outlying districts, including Meltham. As the children from Meltham required four buses, the Education Committee's minutes show that serious consideration was given to starting a train from the village, even though it had lost its passenger services ten years earlier. In June of 1959 BR wrote "a train service from Meltham, calling at Netherton, Berry Brow, Honley, Thongsbridge and Holmfirth, would only be feasible once sufficient supplies of the diesel railcars became available." Another service was also being investigated from Clayton West and Skelmanthorpe to Honley and Holmfirth, calling at Shepley, Stocksmoor, Brockholes and Thongsbridge.

Yet in June 1959, BR issued their proposals to withdraw passenger services on the branch. Holmfirth Council in turn received notification early in July that a meeting of the Transport Users' Consultative Committee would be held on 1st September 1959. The *Huddersfield Examiner* reported on this on 21st August, with the headline DON'T STOP RAIL SERVICE - GIVE US DIESELS.

The council said, "inadequate though the present service is, the trains are now carrying more passengers than at any time for the past ten years. The demand for the present service is bound to grow, and it is not unreasonable to assume that a more adequate service would result in the growth of demand being even greater." It is surprising to read that, although one arm of BR was aware of the new school services then being proposed, that the British Transport Commission was not aware of this when they announced their closure proposals.

These were not the only 'False Facts' that BR had submitted about the branch, as the *Huddersfield Examiner* went on to show in a report it carried four days later. According to Councillor F. Higson, who was to lead the TUCC deputation hearing, "there was a risk of a grave miscarriage of justice to the community of the Holme Valley." Following the receipt of the closure notice, Holmfirth Council had had the opportunity to study the figures most carefully and had found the passenger train situation "nowhere near as grave as had been first suggested." Parcels traffic from Holmfirth was extremely lucrative, but the £6,000 annual revenue from this was not shown anywhere in the figures. It was further claimed that "information in that [the closure] memorandum is totally misleading, and certainly the facts are false."

Another of the facts the Council believed to be untrue concerned the replacement bus services, as no provision could be made on these for mothers with prams. The Council also wondered, if the proposals would have been made if "the Transport Commission had not had a half share in buses running from Huddersfield to Holmfirth?" There was no competition, only collusion, so was the service being condemned to death on false evidence?

Nevertheless, despite the petitions, protests and objections from Holmfirth, Honley and New Mill councils, West Riding County Council and the Education Committee, the TUCC rubber-stamped the BTC closure, stating that the HJOC, Yorkshire Traction and the West Riding Automobile Company could provide adequate alternate bus services.

Yet, even the local bus operators Baddeley Brothers had said that bus services should be co-ordinated with the railway and not used to replace it. The council therefore appealed against the Yorkshire Area TUCC's decision ! However, the appropriately named General Sir Roy Bucher) of The Central User's Transport Consultative Committee then wrote: "The Government [Conservative] had repeatedly indicated the desirability of withdrawing un-remunerative facilities, unless it could be proved hardship would be caused." The staggering losses that BR said it was sustaining amounted to £7,439pa, but they also admitted that once dieselised, this would drop to a loss of £4,000pa.

Given that the £6,000 a year generated by parcels traffic was attributed to Huddersfield station's receipts, the true fact meant that the line was profitable. A request for a year's moratorium whilst the schools traffic and the DMU services began was also turned down.

Yet, demand for travel remained high, on Saturday 26th September, a special left the branch with 500 passengers on a 'Honley Feast' excursion. Steam trains operated passenger services right up to the last day, although diesel multiple unit services had already started on the Penistone line for the 1959 winter timetable. Saturday 31st October 1959 saw 2-6-4T 42116 leave Holmfirth at 4.53pm, with many passengers boarding it to make a round trip. The final train left Huddersfield at 5.26pm behind 42413 with the coaches fully packed. To compound the misery for local people, Huddersfield Town also lost by a solitary goal in the 'derby match' with Sheffield Wednesday.

Demand from Holmfirth people was high as crowds thronged to join the last train out of the town, even though they had to catch the bus back. Maureen Jessop recalls that her father took a trip to Thongsbridge and walked home.

As the last train went over Mytholm Bridge Viaduct, cascades of fireworks were thrown from the carriage windows as a passing salute to the branch. David Robertson of Horbury was then a 16-year old from Lockwood and recalls that he and his friend emulated the cascade at Lockwood Viaduct, but by Thornton Lodge the pyrotechnics were all gone, so rolls of toilet paper from the train lavatory were pressed into service.

The driver of the last train, Bob Wilson from Low Moor could not understand the withdrawal. Of the closure he said "there had been a good number of passengers using the trains, and we thought that diesels might have been good for the branch and helped to keep it alive."

Top Left: *Sadly the plans to use DMUs on services to Holmfirth never came to fruition, even though the station name was printed on the new destination blinds. Here a two-car Metro-Cammell set heads through Honley in October 1959 en-route for driver-training on the branch.* Francis Bray

Middle Left: *An RCTS 'special' in September 1964 is often quoted as the last passenger train. Yet, on 28th April 1965 a 'school charter' left the branch in a DMU. It returned on Saturday 1st May, and is seen here as it passes on to the branch at Brockholes Junction.* Francis Bray

Bottom Left: *A view of a three-car DMU as it leaves Honley on 16th August 1986 shows that DMUs kept the H&JR route alive, even though stations en-route were all made into unmanned halts. From Colour-Rail transparency D597.*

FREIGHT TRAFFIC

Freight traffic was always intensive, and from the early days it was this traffic that was seen as the *raison-d'eter*. Holmfirth provided a lucrative source of woollen goods as outward traffic, and had a voracious demand for coal as incoming traffic.

Above: *Although this section covers freight traffic, this picture (taken in June 1959) of 2-6-2T 42158 shows that the goods yard still looks extremely busy only a few months before the withdrawal of the passenger services. Although partially obscured by smoke from the Ivatt tank, the cattle dock can be made out, whilst the sleeper-built loading dock is clearly visible.* J. Davenport

Top Left: *Two roads served the top of the coal drops, and these were protected by a sleeper-built deck. A paved cartway led down to the warehouse. A three-ton yard crane was also once located at the northern end of the coal drops.*

Bottom Left: *In 1887 improvements were made to the goods yard, with the erection of stables, weighbridge and offices for the coal merchants. This view from 1962 looks down the approach road towards Bridge Lane, with the coal merchant's offices on the right, followed by the weigh machine and garage/stables.*

A large goods yard was provided at the terminus, and in its final form Holmfirth could hold 113 wagons, whilst Thongsbridge could take 44. The goods arrangement was difficult to work however, as all incoming trains had to use the platform line, before shunting could begin. The coal business was particularly strong and the coal drops made use of the natural fall of the land to create a system where coals were dropped by gravity.

In some cases coal would be dropped directly into a waiting road vehicle. But in the days of horse carts this practice was soon condemned by the Blue Cross Society, who were concerned with the welfare of horses, as the shock of coal hitting the bed of the cart was transmitted down the shafts and onto the animal's back. Consequently most of the coal would be shovelled in the carts by hand.

In total 12 cells were provided, and these were let to local merchants. Firms like Benjamin Hardy and Armitage's (later Deakin & Crosland) had their own private-owner wagons, as did the Holmfirth Co-operative Society and the Gas Light company.

Other merchants (Howarth, Lockwood and Whiteley) were chiefly supplied by a regular working from Skelmanthorpe station on the Clayton West branch. This was a twice weekly (thrice in winter) working from the Emley Moor Colliery of Sir John L. Kaye, Baronet. The livery for these private-owner wagons was an attractive royal blue with shaded white lettering. By the 1880s there was a seven-train goods service (Monday to Friday), but this then dropped to five after World War I . At least one of these workings was an 'express goods' that was either fully or partially fitted and conveyed bales of finished textiles to Manchester or Liverpool.

During World War I, there was huge growth in woollen cloth traffic as large quantities of finished un-dyed cloth were 'imported' from the Dewsbury area, and sent to the local dye works for the production of 'khaki'. In February 1916 all the parcels traffic destined for Penistone was sent to Holmfirth for movement by road, when the Penistone Viaduct collapse severed the H&JR line. After the war, the Holmfirth goods traffic remained high, but during the 'Depression' it declined to four trains each day. However the branch did return to a five-train daily freight service by 1937 and this was maintained throughout World War II.

Right: *These views reveal that there were 12 coal cells located on the approach road, each of which was identified by a cast-iron number. However the picture on page 21 shows that the two coal roads had originally 15 apertures below. The set of steps and hand rails are also later additions, as the aforementioned picture shows a different original arrangement.*

Top Left: *The coal drops had been taken out of use by the time this picture was taken in 1962 and the cattle dock has lost its pens and been turned into a loading mound for the coal merchant. A three-ton Ford tipper lorry sits at a crazy angle on the dock, and beyond it the coal merchant has started having his supplies just tipped out on to the sidings and paved cartway.*

Bottom Left: *This is the remaining yard crane at Holmfirth in 1962, as the one in the goods shed and the one by the coal drops had by then both been removed.*

Gordon Ellis remembers, that in the 1950s: "There was always the likelihood of coal being delivered to the yard by road. This had to be watched carefully as there was a special charge for these deliveries being left in the goods yard. The goods clerk was usually available to 'collar' the lorry driver and get details of the load, so a bill could be given to the merchant. There were numerous piles of coal in the yard belonging to the various merchants and these were added to on each delivery – by either road or rail.

Everyone knew the conditions but it became a game for a driver to drop his load and speed off down the access road before being apprehended. Once the load had been dropped it was almost impossible to identify one heap of coal from another, and the coal merchant would flatly deny that any had arrived by road. All the station staff were on the lookout and if a lorry was spotted the call would go to the goods clerk - 'roadborne!' If he were not available then another member of staff would try and get the details. Sometimes the lorry driver won!"

Special campaigns were also run at various times, most notably in the early 1950s during the building of the Digley reservoir near Holme. This saw a fleet of 14 BR 'Sundries' road vehicles being transferred to Holmfirth, where they were based to convey materials between the railhead and the construction site. The other big campaign proved to be an even more arduous task, as this involved moving large quantities of steelwork from the station yard to the top of Holme Moss in connection with the construction of the new BBC Television station and mast.

The first casualty was actually noted with declining freight trends in the textile traffic, particularly 'pieces' or large bales of woollen cloth after the end of hostilities in 1945. Most firms had, by then, invested in the purchase of motor lorries to carry their produce to the wholesale warehouses in Huddersfield, Manchester and Leeds.

The woollen piece warehouse was little used after the end of World War II and it is believed to have been finally demolished by the autumn of 1956. The other warehouse remained open for general traffic but it seems to have gone out of use in or around 1960; thereafter parcels were handled from the passenger station.

A former goods clerk at this warehouse recalls a case of pilferage that he had to investigate concerning a case of whisky. "The case had been delivered some months before to a private house, but as the man consumed his stock of whisky he discovered that some of the bottles only contained cold tea. The clerk took the waybill back to the station, and from this the company checked back to all the locations where the case had been handled on its route south.

Water samples were taken at all these locations, and by a process of elimination it was discovered that the water in the tea did not match any of these places in fact, to the contrary, the water matched identically with that from the distillery. The pilferage had occurred not in transit, but at the source."

Top Right: *One of the special forms of 'special campaign traffic' was the large metal pipes and valves that were shipped to Holmfirth in the late 1940s and early 1950s. Steven Wood, whose uncle ran the cartage from the station writes: "The pipes were quite huge and mostly came from the Sheffield area in connection with the building of the Digley Reservoir", a project that is seen here whilst under construction.* Huddersfield Examiner

Bottom Right: *Although this is a somewhat grainy shot, this 1958 view from Holmfirth Signal Cabin shows a little photographed part of the station; namely the low-level loading dock and crane by the coal drops. Note the timber staging and the loading bay lamp complete with ladder.* Harold Armitage

It is surprising to note that livestock traffic was also an early casualty despite the extensive agricultural area that surrounded the town. The cattle dock was stripped of its pens in 1960 and sometime shortly afterwards the coal drops were taken out of service. Looking at the load-bearing timbers in 1962, it was easy to see that they had been deteriorating for some time and this was probably the reason for their progressive removal from service. After the passenger trains ended in 1959 there was still a twice-daily freight service, but in 1961 the branch was singled and given a 20mph speed limit.

Locomotives employed on freight trains in the 1950s were 7F 0-8-0s, ex-WD 0-8-0s and 3F 0-6-0s. But Stanier Black 5s or 2-8-0s and Hughes 2-6-0 (Crabs), were seen along with 2-6-4 and 2-6-2 tanks. In April 1965 a Type 4 diesel (class 40) D259, ran driver-training tests along the branch and sidings at Holmfirth. A few days later on 28th April, Stanier 8F 48305, hauled away the last few remaining empty wagons.

Francis Bray recalls that the track-lifting was a sporadic affair, which took place during the summer of 1965 and then stopped abruptly. He states that it re-commenced in the spring of 1966, when road lorries took away the last of the sleepers and cut down sections of rail from Thongsbridge goods yard. Various, but contradictory dates have been given to me about the demolition of the station buildings at the intermediary station, but none have been positively confirmed.

Top Left: *Pictures of the Holmfirth Signal Cabin are few and far between, although one view of the front of the 'box appears in the Lancashire & Yorkshire Railway Society's excellent little booklet on the branch. This picture shows Harold Armitage at the cabin during the 1950s, but it will be noted that the nameboard has already 'gone missing' from above the door.* Harold Armitage

Bottom Left: *The view from the signal cabin looking across to the timber crossing over the two lines leading to the coal drops. The view shows the end of the low-level timber stage, the goods yard 'no trespassing sign' and a coal merchant's office. The vehicle looks very much like a late model Bedford WT series truck. Whilst retaining the cab of the WT model, the front cowl is of the type that would be fitted to the Bedford O-Type when it was introduced in 1939. Presumably, it is here being used by one of the local coal merchants.* Harold Armitage

MEMORIES OF THE GREAT WAR AND AFTER

During the war the small hospitals at Holmfirth and Dean Royd were used to house wounded soldiers, so in June 1916 the branch saw the arrival of an Ambulance train comprised of Midland Railway stock drawn by a Great Central 4-4-0 locomotive. It is not clear how the engine worked back south after its trip to Holmfirth, as it would have been both too large and too heavy for the turntable.

Above: *They say that a picture is worth a thousand words, and here we have one that really shouts out to those who said the L&YR never operated their own lorries in Holmfirth. Obviously heading towards the station, this is an ex-US Army Peerless truck, which had been purchased by the L&YR as military surplus after World War I. Although the houses on the right of Towngate have long since been demolished, generations of local people will recognise Swallow's Ironmonger's on the left, which later became Kaye's.*

Top Left: *We do not have any views of ambulance trains at Holmfirth, but this is a view of St. George's Square, Huddersfield in 1916. During a three-day period over 7,000 filed past the George Hotel (far right) and the Peel statue to visit the L&YR Ambulance Train Exhibition, which was located in the bay platform at the LNWR end of the station.*

Bottom Left: *This view shows a scene recalled by Mr. Ludlam, when the Low Moor Chemical Works exploded near Bradford. Railway workers trained in 'ambulance work' were rushed there from all over the L&YR system, including many from Holmfirth, three of whom won medals from the L&YR thanks to their unstinting work. John Gartside of Underbank, a travelling ticket inspector also received a Humane Society award, who despite sustaining terrible chemical burns on his hands continued in the rescue work. The destruction to the rolling stock at Low Moor shows the ferocity of the fireball that swept across the tracks.*
Both L&YR Official

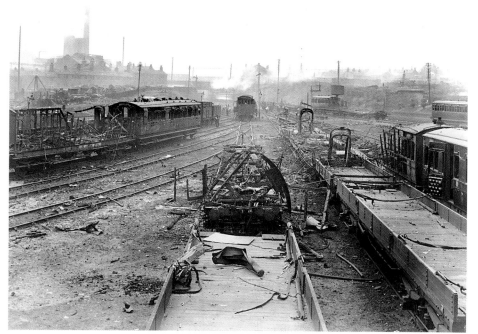

Francis Bray, whose father and uncles worked on the Holmfirth branch, recalls having been taken as a small boy to watch its arrival. "It pulled into the station about nine at night, and though it was bitterly cold there must have been about a hundred folk on the platform, most of them mill girls with nowt on bar a dress and a shawl. Most had a bag with fruit, sweets or a pouch of 'baccy to give the wounded soldiers. They knew none of them, but if their menfolk were hurting at some strange town then they hoped that other folk would be just as kind to them."

He also remembers how the working went, saying "the next passenger train were due in a bit after nine, but it were cancelled, or at least only went as far as Brockholes for it never came down the branch at all. Next thing to come was the ambulance train. There were a lot of folk waiting to go to Huddersfield but they all mixed in with the helpers. I had newspapers handed to me to give out, and I remember how pleased the soldiers were when I took them round.

I helped sweep out coaches in which the wounded had been sat so they could send the waiting passengers to Brockholes where they'd catch a train from Penistone. But they couldn't put the engine over the turntable, so it had to push the coaches in front of it back down the line."

However, visits by ambulance trains were very rare , and it seems that only two other such workings were seen during the war. This hardly accords with War Department records that state that "a constant flow of war-wounded was sent to Holmfirth, Dean House and No.17 Temporary Convalescent Hospital." Notices in the traffic orders do seem to indicate that once the hospitals had been initially filled, any vacated beds were given to patients who were conveyed from Huddersfield either by road ambulance or in special coaches attached to branch services.

During the war Holmfirth (in common with all manned L&YR stations in the area) was used as a Reporting Centre for the wounded that had been discharged to their own homes to recover. Once a week the soldier or sailor would be directed to submit a telegraph signal to his home port or RHQ, whereby a doctor's certificate would confirm his continuing incapacity. The railway companies were used as the agency to send this signal in preference to the GPO, as they had direct links (via the Railway Executive's offices in Westminster) to all the various military establishments.

This work soon became too great for the railways to undertake, and it was later amended to a more workable arrangement via post offices. Only those men who were known malingerers were thereafter to report to railway or police stations, so that their 'sick notes' might be examined.

Life at Holmfirth in the last few years of the Great War was related to me by Mr. A. J. Ludlam OBE of South Africa who travelled back to the Holme Valley to meet me in 1991. His story is a fascinating one as he had been appointed as a boy telegraphist at Brockholes Station in 1917.

However, just after he had taken up his post the telegraph system was replaced by telephone after the National Telephone Company had been nationalised as part of the General Post Office. He was then offered the post of clerk due to the great shortage of men who had been 'called up' for military service. He related that "throughout the district most of the administrative posts on the railway had been filled by the young, the old, those unfit for service and some women.

The shortages of staff meant that those of us who remained had to become general factotums at an early age, and this was true with my work as a clerk at Holmfirth. One week I would be working as the goods clerk, the next I would be the booking office clerk and I had to be able to do anything. In the booking office I usually issued a minimum of 250 weekly Workman's Tickets on the 05.38 to Huddersfield. The fare was 2s 6d (12.5p) for six return journeys, but you had to travel outwards before 08.00 and not return home until after 16.00.

Another busy period was when we sold Market-return tickets (Tuesdays and Saturdays), which cost 8d (3.5p) as opposed to the normal return fare of one shilling (5p). I often booked more than 200 'market-day' returns but the trouble was that people never came early, and by 12.40 there was a real queue that spilled out into the street, so you really had to move before the 12.50 pulled out.

The work of a goods clerk was most interesting, as I found that I had to handle a good deal of 'claims work'. These claims were mostly from recipients complaining about short delivery or pilferage. One day I was called upon to go and see a shopkeeper about 'shortages' in a crate containing boxes of chocolates from a well-known manufacturer in York.

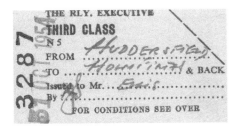
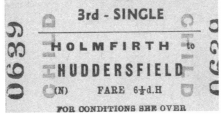

We examined the contents of the crate and checked these against the manufacturers invoice for 20 boxes but there were only 18 within. The man was perplexed because, to all intents and purposes, the packing case looked outwardly perfect and there was no room for the missing 2lb boxes. So he was forced to agree with my view that it must have been a case of short packing at the factory, but then I saw the railway's consignment note (waybill). This was endorsed "re-packed at Thornhill". I subsequently discovered that at this trans-ship station the L&YR had a special department for mending and repairing damaged packages, such as our case of chocolates. If a box was discovered open, broken either by accident or intent, then it would be repaired before being sent on to the recipient.

Expert carpenters based at Thornhill would strip down the case or box, and then re-build it so the contents that remained just filled the packing. In doing so, the company prevented further loss or pilferage, in addition to protecting the remaining items from possible damage caused by movement in a part empty box. It was common practice for the joiners to leave one side intact this usually being the side with the sender's lettering on it."

Interestingly, in our conversation I mentioned a model railway layout based on Holmfirth Station that I built for exhibition. At the time I had been taken to task by several 'commentators' who criticised me for having an L&YR motor lorry on the layout based on Holmfirth. "The L&YR", they said "never had any motorised vehicles at Holmfirth and suggested I should have known better!"

I had to concede that since the opening of the line, the delivery of goods or passengers' parcels was done by a firm of local haulage contractors. This firm did use horse drawn vehicles (some owned by the railway) and rented stables from the L&YR, which were located on the lane leading down from the station yard.

Yet, Mr. Ludlam related there had been a change in the delivery services, saying: - "The contractors in 1918 were Middleton Brothers, who exclusively handled all the L&YR traffic over a large area and were paid at a fixed rate. This was worked out by the company who gave free delivery to customers for anything within a radius of one mile, an extra amount was charged for deliveries up to two miles, whilst anything beyond that distance had an even higher charge. Though the first mile was covered by the L&YR, any charges for additional mileage were a matter between the contractor and the recipient.

Up to 1916 the charges and rates had roughly remained the same, as had wages and rents, but during the war (when price increases became a frequent occurrence) the contractor had asked for, and received, regular increases in his tariff. By 1919 it had become his habit to ask for more at the end of each December and June, notifying the L&YR he needed the increase or he would have to stop collecting and delivering. Midway through 1920 he gave one month's notice of another hike in his prices, but this time he did not get a reply from Manchester as he had always done.

On the last day of July a worried Joe Middleton came up to see Stationmaster Moxon, and the three of us were stood on the platform outside the office discussing the possible reasons why the L&YR had not replied to his notice. From where we were stood you could see the road from Huddersfield quite clearly, and as we talked a procession of five or six goods vehicles were coming along the road towards Holmfirth. Not many minutes later all the vehicles pulled up in the station yard opposite. All were brand new, and all were boldly lettered LYR and Mr Moxon said "Well Joe - there's your answer!"

The man in charge asked Mr Moxon to inform the contractor to vacate his premises immediately so that they could be used for garaging the new motor vehicles, and that, from thereon the company would be doing it's own carting. Mr Ludlam said, "Never before or since have I ever heard anything to compare with Mr. Middleton's outburst!" All the lorries, except a Leyland 1-ton parcel van, were brand new Peerless 4-toners, which had been bought as surplus from the American Army stores near Liverpool. As there had been very few motor lorries in the area before and never any on the railway, Mr Ludlam said:

"It was fortunate that the Labour Exchange were able to help us. There had been quite a few local men who had learned to drive in the army, and having recently been demobilised they had just signed-on.' The development of the railway's road service really took off after 1921 and was helped along by these war surplus vehicles, which were assigned to work from all the outlying stations in the L&YR's Huddersfield district. They changed the whole scene as drastically as the development of the railways in the 19th Century had led to the decline of canals and turnpikes. Middleton's survived and started a local garage alongside the haulage business. When he retired Mr. Moxon bought a plot of land off the LMS and built a house alongside the track between the station and Berry Banks!"

POSTSCRIPT

Time does not stand still, and today the branch line to Holmfirth is unrecognisable for what it once was, and the chance of ever re-building it has surely passed us by.

The line was dismantled in 1966, and for years the station at Holmfirth stood a derelict eyesore, despite my attempts to buy it in 1971 and 1972. According to a letter sent to me by the BR Property Board, the asking price was a mere £2,875 but I couldn't afford it then. It was eventually sold for £3,685 to a property developer, and even then little was done with it. In 1979 it went back on the market at £15,000 but the single storey buildings had become so badly vandalised, that they were demolished.

Above: *The re-development of part of the site, saw a new stone-built church constructed by an army of 2,500 volunteers in just one weekend from start to finish.* Glyn Thomas

The lovely station looked well past its best, but the grime-covered and derelict Stationmaster's house, complete with its mock Tudor chimneys was later fully refurbished and turned into an attractive house once again. The goods warehouse also became a family home, and new houses were built on the goods yard. In the early 1980s plans for the station site came and went, but in August 1985 the local congregation of Jehovah's Witnesses, built a Kingdom Hall church on the site of the single storey passenger buildings and put a car park on the track-bed.

Top Left: *After doing some site preparation in the early part of 1985, the Jehovah's Witnesses set about building a church on the site in one weekend. An army of volunteers, mostly skilled craftsmen who were members of the faith, congregated on the old station site. This view shows work progressing on the Kingdom Hall, whilst the former goods shed on the right is also under conversion but by a much slower process.*

Bottom Left: *The work on the Kingdom Hall was finished by late Sunday afternoon, and the building was ready in time for a service to be held inside that night.*

Moving away from Holmfirth, the land around Berry Banks was used for industrial purposes for many years, first of all by Dougie Naylor's plant hire business. It was here that I both learned to drive, thanks to my schoolboy friend John Naylor and an old Wylis Jeep, and also had my altercation with their dog. In more recent times, the site is more likely to be associated with Wells & Moorhouse scrap merchants.

In recent times several proposals to develop the land for housing have failed to come to fruition, but at the time of writing approval has been finally granted to a firm of developers. Land clearance had begun in the late summer of 2003, and another part of railway local history has now become buried under concrete, brick and stone.

Thongsbridge goods station yard was developed as a housing estate several years ago, and the passenger station site has been partially filled in at either end, although the upper section of steps from Heys Road are still there. The viaduct over New Mill Beck was demolished over a quarter of a century ago, but large chunks of masonry can still be seen littering the bed of the valley.

Keith Hollingworth, who has helped with the research for this book, tells me there is still the shoulder of one arch resting where it fell. Examination thereof clearly shows how the viaduct was constructed back in 1866-7.

Gone then, but not forgotten, the branch holds many memories for a wide spectrum of people. The pictures herein, will of course refresh those memories, and I am grateful to the people who have kindly loaned material for inclusion.

A number of the views in this book are credited to the firm of Bamforth & Co. who produced postcards in Holmfirth from the 1880s on. This firm also produced silent films and these were so popular they were exported around the world. World War I eventually put an end to film production, but the company then started making romantic postcards that sold well during the war. In later years, they became better known for their range of saucy postcards.

Talking of local pictures, can I make an appeal to those readers who have any views of local railways (including the Holmfirth branch). If you would like to share them with other readers, I'd be delighted to hear from you care of the Appleby address at the front of this book.

Top Right: *Although much of the H&SJR has been reduced to single track, this 1987 view shows Brockholes is still served by two tracks as a Metro-Cammell two-car DMU heads towards Huddersfield. Private housing has occupied the old goods yard, whilst the Stationmaster's house has also passed out of railway use and become a private dwelling.*

Bottom Right: *The station at Brockholes eventually made a desirable residence, but the junction they were built to serve no longer exists. This view in 1986 shows the rear elevation, which had changed little!*

Above: *Brockholes Station, where a flower pot (below the Way Out sign) has been made from a length of old drain pipe and the rim off 661 , the Aspinall 2-4-2T that fell from Penistone Viaduct when it collapsed. The station was also the place where two or three six-wheeled coaches were 'slipped' from Holmfirth or Penistone trains and then worked up to Clayton West by either the 'Brockholes Pilot' or the 'Clayton West Pilot'; both of which came up to do their respective duties on a daily basis from Mirfield Shed. However, this was a continuous source of trouble, with many runaways occurring. In turn some of these incidents led to both the complete destruction of the stock involved and the condemnation of the Board of Trade. By the time this picture was taken in 1964, the station had changed out of all recognition and the Holmfirth trains had been withdrawn. Yet, despite this, the notice boards have barely changed and they give an impression that it is still an L&YR station. Eric Blakey*

With sincere thanks and acknowledgement to:

Jack Adamson
the late Frank Alcock
Harold Armitage
Bamforths Ltd.
A. J. A. Bastable
British Rail
Colin Battye
Francis & Doris Bray
Colour Rail
Gordon Ellis
Kenneth Field
Keith Hollingworth
Holme Valley Express
House of Lords Records

Huddersfield Examiner
Alvin Iredale
Kirklees MBC
the late David Jenkinson
Barry C. Lane
Arthur Ludlam
National Monuments
Gavin Morrison
National Railway Museum
Ian Stringer
Brian Stott
Peter Sunderland
Glyn Thomas
the late Eric Treacy